Five Simple
Ways
to Grow a
Great Family

Five Simple Ways to Grow a Great Family

CAROL KUYKENDALL

SPIRE

© 2005 by Carol Kuykendall

Published by Revell
a division of Baker Publishing Group
P.O. Box 6287, Grand Rapids, MI 49516-6287
www.revellbooks.com

Spire edition published 2008
ISBN 978-0-8007-8761-5

Previously published under the title *Five Star Families*

Printed in the United States of America

Unless otherwise indicated, Scripture is taken from the HOLY BIBLE, NEW INTERNATIONAL VERSION®. NIV®. Copyright © 1973, 1978, 1984 by International Bible Society. Used by permission of Zondervan. All rights reserved.

Scripture marked CEV is taken from the Contemporary English Version © 1991, 1992, 1995 by American Bible Society. Used by permission.

Scripture marked GNT is taken from the Good News Translation—Second Edition Copyright © 1992 by American Bible Society. Used by permission.

Scripture marked KJV is taken from the King James Version of the Bible.

Scripture marked TLB is taken from *The Living Bible*, copyright © 1971. Used by permission of Tyndale House Publishers, Inc., Wheaton, Illinois 60189. All rights reserved.

Scripture marked Message is taken from *The Message* by Eugene H. Peterson, copyright © 1993, 1994, 1995, 2000, 2001, 2002. Used by permission of NavPress Publishing Group. All rights reserved.

Scripture marked NLT is taken from the *Holy Bible*, New Living Translation, copyright © 1996. Used by permission of Tyndale House Publishers, Inc., Wheaton, Illinois 60189. All rights reserved.

Scripture marked RSV is taken from the Revised Standard Version of the Bible, copyright 1952 [2nd edition, 1971] by the Division of Christian Education of the National Council of the Churches of Christ in the United States of America. Used by permission. All rights reserved.

Published in association with the literary agency of Alive Communications, Inc., 7680 Goddard Street, Suite 200, Colorado Springs, Colorado 80920.

To my family—with gratitude
for all you have taught me

Contents

Prologue: How I Wonder . . . 9
Introduction: Memo to Mom 11

Part 1   Family Matters

1 Family Beginnings: We're a FAMILY!   19
2 Family Dreams: What Kind of Family Do We Want to Be?   37
3 Family Surprises: Wow! Children Bring Us "Gifts"!   53

**Part 2   What Matters Most:
            Aiming for Five-Star Qualities**

4 Love: Love Meets Our Greatest Needs   67
5 Fun: Fun Makes Us Want to Be Together   87
6 Loyalty: Loyalty Connects Us . . . for Always   109
7 Growth: Growing Keeps Us Healthy   131
8 Faith: Faith Lights Our Way Home   153
9 Full-Circle Families   173

Epilogue   187
Acknowledgments   189

Prologue

How I Wonder . . .

My daughter Lindsay just called from California.

She and her husband are expecting their first child in a few months, so they are making preparations.

"Mom, can you send me some of my baby pictures?" she asked.

Her simple question reminded me of my own preparations when my husband, Lynn, and I were expecting our first child a generation earlier. All of a sudden, I had a new interest in my baby pictures. I wanted to compare and connect and fit this new baby into our larger family picture. Kind of like putting pieces of a puzzle together.

I especially remember my favorite childhood picture of myself. It's now on the wall of our bedroom in a collage of family pictures. An old, black-and-white photo in a simple, oval, gold frame. I'm probably three years old, a chubby little girl wearing a polka-dotted dress, kneeling on the hardwood surface of a deep bay window that served as my make-believe stage. From that spot, I could look into our home, which felt secure—or out through the white-paned window into the wondrous world beyond our family.

In this picture, I'm kneeling down and singing my signature song from that season of my life. . . .

> Twinkle, twinkle, little star,
> How I wonder what you are.
> Up above the world so high,
> Like a diamond in the sky.
> Twinkle, twinkle, little star,
> How I wonder what you are.

How many times I looked out that bay window at night and saw twinkling stars lighting the black velvet sky. And wondered about things I didn't know.

I still love that picture today because it embraces what family represents to me—a safe and stretching place from which to grow and wonder.

As my daughter prepares for their first child, she is creating a vision for her own family. She and her husband will collect baby pictures, which will stir up their own childhood memories. They will set up a crib and fill the changing table with tiny diapers. They will dream and make plans and sometimes wonder what matters most in the midst of it all.

It is for my daughter—and all the other mothers of her generation—that I write this book.

Introduction

Memo to Mom

Hello . . . mom. Are you there?

I know you're busy and you have a lot of things on your mind. That's called "normal" in a mom's life. But I have a quick question: *what matters most in the midst of all you're doing?*

I've been asking lots of moms that question, and the overwhelming answer is "my family." Yes! Family matters— because family is that circle of people who mean the most to us in the whole wide world. People, bound by birth or choice, whom we almost always love, even when we don't always like them. Family makes our lives matter.

But if family matters to you, have you thought about what kind of family you want to be?

Loving? Fun? Loyal? Growing? Faithful?

Those answers remind me of the words that popped off the magazine cover I got in the mail recently. "Want a flatter belly? Stronger arms? Firmer thighs?" What no-brainers! Of course my answer is a resounding "Yes!" But I didn't even open the magazine, because I felt sure it would tell me that—in order to get what I wanted—I would have to bound out of bed every morning, hit the floor, and do one hundred full-body crunches before even drinking a cup of coffee. And actually, I shouldn't even drink that cup of coffee. Or eat that bagel. Or have any chocolate in the house.

No thanks!

I can't live like that. And I sure don't need one more guilt trip. But give me some options. Like, tell me how to strengthen my stomach muscles at red lights or thin my thighs with leg lifts while talking on the phone (I love multitasking). Give me some doable ideas that fit into my way of life, and maybe . . . just maybe . . . I'll get an inch or two closer to reaching my goals.

If you ever feel this way, this book is for you! Not because it will flatten your tummy or firm your thighs; it focuses on a deeper longing and need than that. It's about becoming the family you want to be by investing in the relationships that matter most to you in your life. It suggests lots of different, doable ways to do this. You choose the ones that fit your family and your lifestyle. No impossibilities. No guilt trips. Guaranteed!

This book is also written for you, mom, because of the unique *influence* you have on the growth of your family. Notice I didn't say, "because of your *responsibility* for that growth." *Responsibility* would mean the results are up to you. And they are not. The people in your family ultimately make their own choices about their lives. *Influence* means that, as a mom, you help shape the growth of your family.

So what matters most in your family?

I offer the five qualities mentioned earlier: love, fun, loyalty, growth, and faith. Alone, these are just plain good words that are probably part of your family life already. But I'll bet they seem invisible at times. Where is the love on a rainy Saturday afternoon when the kids keep bonking each other on the head? Who cares about fun when you can hardly keep up with the daily necessities of feeding, wiping, laundering, and carpooling (to name only a few of those necessities)? You get the picture. These qualities often seem invisible in the reality of our lives.

That's the point. (Five points, actually!) The process of becoming a five-star family happens in the midst of maneuvering our way through the bumps in our lives. I remember endlessly telling our children to be kind to each other ("No more teasing!"), say "please" and "thank you" ("What's the magic word?"), quit whining ("I can't hear you in that voice"), and not say "hate" ("We hate that word!").

My efforts seemed invisible.

Then I'd catch a glimpse of an older brother reaching out for the hand of his younger sister as we crossed a parking lot. Or a three-year-old thanking my friend for a cookie, without even being told. Or a first grader choosing to play with the child nobody else plays with at recess. In these moments, the invisible

---

Family means…

Not having to speak to be heard.

---

becomes visible, like a star that begins to twinkle and shine in the evening sky.

In these moments, our families begin to shine. We go from good to great!

This shine process takes some perseverance. Any worthwhile effort does. But it's the most important investment we can make, especially when our children are young and our influence is the greatest.

And the process begins with us first. As you know, the family is the primary place of growth in our lives. It is the context in which we discover the most about ourselves. So if we want our families to shine with love, fun, loyalty, growth, and faith, we need to examine these qualities in our own lives. For instance,

Love: what expressions of love make you feel most loved?

Fun: what kind of fun recharges your own batteries?

Loyalty: what does healthy family loyalty mean to you?

Growth: how are you continuing to grow, even though you're grown-up?

Faith: where do you find the kind of hope that you can shine into the lives of the people in your family?

As we discover the depth of these qualities in our own lives, we recognize the ways we can influence these qualities' life-shaping growth in our family members.

You matter, mom. And your influence in your family matters, especially in those early years when the foundation of your family is being set.

On a more personal note, I'm writing this book because family matters to me and I'm at a place of new perspective in my life. Lynn and I have raised three children who are grown and married and starting families of their own. I now see a bigger picture. I have a clearer view of what matters most. And what doesn't.

The great surprise of this new season is the joy of having a new generation of babies being born into our family, creating new families, new relationships, new love. New children who will look up at the night sky and sing, "Twinkle, Twinkle, Little Star."

Mom, I know you are busy. But this book is written with your lifestyle in mind. You can read it in bite-size pieces that will fit into your time frames. Sprinkled throughout, you'll find one-line definitions of family from other mothers just like you.

Hopefully, as you read, you will begin to see the ways you can influence your family to experience and express these five qualities. When you do, you bring out the best in each other. And you grow closer to God's dream for us as individuals and families . . . that we might "shine like stars in the universe" (Phil. 2:15).

Wow!

Family Matters

1

Family Beginnings

We're a FAMILY!

We're a FAMILY!

Do you remember the moment that realization first hit you?

For me, it was not the moment I held our firstborn late that night in the delivery room with my husband, Lynn, by my side. As much as I expected that to be a magical maternal moment, I mostly remember shaking uncontrollably and feeling oddly disconnected from the baby now being weighed and measured by a nurse nearby.

It was not even the next morning when I finally unswaddled him from his blanket and stared at his eight-pound, five-ounce body in amazement! Not only at the miracle of his perfect fingers and toes, but his huge (still cone-shaped) head. *He . . . came through me!* No wonder I could hardly move!

Instead, it was two days later when we brought our baby home from the hospital. We lived in a small rental unit in San Diego, where Lynn was in the Navy. My parents had just arrived, driving all the way from Colorado. They were busy unpacking their suitcases in the spare bedroom upstairs. (This was to be an open-ended stay!) I was feeling a bit more normal and less traumatized, stretched out on the couch, bassinet at my side, where our baby slept peacefully. After helping to carry the suitcases upstairs, Lynn plopped down at the end of the couch and repositioned my feet on his lap. Together, we gazed at our baby.

A wave of euphoria washed over me in a moment I will never forget. *We're a FAMILY!*

Of course my emotions went on a roller-coaster ride over the next few days, weeks, and years. Euphoria mixed with reality. Like surprising postpartum moodiness. And feelings of *Yikes! Help! Wow!* And lots more.

In those first few days, I struggled to find my footing in this new place between my mother on one side and our new baby on the other. Did I trust my mother to give the baby a bath? What if she didn't do it the way I learned at the hospital? Could I teach her? Who's the grown-up here? The questions and highs and lows went on and on.

We're a FAMILY! That's a heady realization, and in the beginning, we hardly understand how an eight-pound infant can transform the dynamics of our whole family and our whole lives. Not that we're not warned. A protruding belly often invites words of advice, so most of us experience a scene similar to this:

I'm standing in the checkout line at the discount store, buying a bunch of newborn-size diapers, about two weeks before my due date. Another mom wheels in behind me with a toddler and an infant in her cart.

"Your first?" she asks, motioning to my belly.

I nod. "Due in two weeks. I can hardly wait."

"Oh," she says, shaking her head with some kind of wisdom I obviously don't have. "Enjoy these last few days. Your life will never be the same."

I don't get her message until a few years later when I'm the one with two children in my cart and I hear myself saying exactly the same thing to a pregnant woman in front of me.

Children change everything. They suddenly fill our world with burp cloths and car seats and passionate new fears about safety and germs. They give us a whole new context from which to live out God's purpose for us in life. They create a whole new circle of roles and relationships. They turn us into parents, our parents into grandparents, our siblings into aunts and uncles. They continue to shape those relationships as we keep discovering what it means to be a family with all the fun and sacrifices and new experiences and messy challenges.

With the news of a pregnancy or an adoption, dreams about the future are born. We enter this new future first by celebrating, which deepens the significance of the milestone, and then by creating a space for our own little family, apart from but within our larger family.

Celebrate!

We're a family! The birth or adoption of your first child— and every addition to your family—gives you a reason to celebrate! A celebration says, "This matters to us, and we are grateful! This is significant!" That's why we celebrate family anniversaries and birthdays and graduations. The observance of family celebrations strengthens a family's foundation.

For some the realization of *We're a family!* comes at the moment of the birth. Or the day you bring the baby home. An adoptive mom says her moment of realization came when she heard her baby crying in a crib that had been empty and prayed over for so many years. A single mom who adopted an older child remembers the realization came to her when she held her child for the first time. The circumstances may be different, but all are the same in significance. *We're a family!*

We're Expecting!

For many, that moment of realization comes much earlier, such as the instant the second blue line crosses the second window in the pregnancy test. And the celebration begins with the important announcement of the news to family and friends.

Some get pretty creative with that news.

One pregnant mom announced the news to her husband by filling his underwear drawer with newborn-size diapers; another by going out for dinner and having his drink delivered in a baby bottle (which takes some negotiating with the waitress!). One couple announced their pregnancy to the husband's family by giving them a bottle of Prego at a family gathering. "How'd you know I needed spaghetti sauce?" his

---

Family means . . .

People who love you and give you room to grow.

---

mom asked, but his sister quickly got the message and started screaming, "They're pregnant!"

Our son, Derek, and his wife, Alexandra, orchestrated an intricate plan to tell us the good news about their first pregnancy. About nine o'clock one frigid January night, the phone rang at our home in Colorado. It was Derek and Alex, calling from their home in Portland. *Not so unusual.*

Lynn and I both got on the phone, and the four of us were talking when our doorbell rang. *Kind of unusual.* It was our thirteen-year-old nephew who lives next door. He handed us a special-delivery package that he said had been left at their house because no one was home at ours.

"What's going on?" Derek asked into the phone, a bit too enthusiastically. *This is starting to get unusual.*

I took one look at the return address on the package (theirs in Portland!) and guessed immediately what was unfolding here. So of course I started crying before we even unwrapped it.

Inside was a light-yellow picture frame with the letters B-A-B-Y across the top and this message:

Dear Grandma and Grandpa,

My mom and dad have been telling me all about you. I can't wait for all the fun things they promise we'll do together at your house, like play with the dogs, go down to the ditch, sled on the hill, and make pancakes. I will see you in September. Until then pray for me and for my parents. (They need it.) I love you.

Baby Kuykendall

It was a holy moment in our family. And a great celebration.

That framed letter was the first of many we received from our grandchild before she was born, reminding us of the love and whimsical joy a baby brings to a family.

One letter came on Mother's Day a few months later, when I received a grandma's brag book. The first page contained a message, accompanied by a copy of the baby's first ultrasound, which looked kind of like an inkblot test until I found the image. Then the picture became profoundly meaningful.

The message read:

Dear Grandma,

You would be proud of me. I have grown so much since these pictures were taken. You can probably tell I look like my dad—and you too! See you soon.

Love, Baby K.

These messages not only bonded us—the grandparents—to our unborn grandchild, they further endeared my daughter-in-law to me as I watched her live out her tender and protective love for their child. She gently caressed her growing belly; she gave up drinking her usual mug of coffee in the morning. She lived differently.

I know that not all prospective grandparents receive the news with enthusiasm, and the parents' announcements may be shaped by the anticipated reaction. "My mom wasn't ready to be called 'grandma,'" one mom said, "so we didn't try to pull off some dramatic way to announce the news."

For some, celebrating the news of the pregnancy with close friends is as important as with extended families. One mom said that she and her husband moved often and left a trail of friends who had been praying for them to have a baby. So she made cards announcing their news and sent them to all their friends. Another mom describes driving over to her girlfriend's home right after she and her husband got the call from the adoption agency that a three-day-old baby was waiting for them. She wanted to share the news in person.

Baby showers also celebrate the family-to-be. (And sometimes educate the mom-to-be!) I attended one recently for my friend Sarah. After playing a guessing game about what kinds of chocolate candy bars had been microwaved into gooey brown messes in several little diapers, we all settled into a circle to watch Sarah open her gifts. With each gift, the giver gave a one-line piece of family advice to this first-time mom:

Trust your instincts.

Watch out when changing diapers . . . poop shoots!

Write down the cute things children say and do. You think you'll never forget, but you do!

A couple times a week, disappear for several hours and leave the baby with daddy, especially during the baby's cranky times, so daddy "gets" it.

Use your mother-in-law.

Learn to ask for help.

Mothering is great, but it's the hardest job you'll ever have.

Establish time-outs, especially for yourself.

And of course . . . the familiar advice that always comes from older moms: enjoy these years; they pass so quickly.

Even more important than the celebration of the pregnancy is the celebration of the birth!

It's a Girl (or Boy)!

A birth announcement tells the world that a new baby has joined the family; it also becomes a unique visual aid with significance that lives beyond the moment. It announces the name the parents have chosen for the baby, which is huge, considering that this name will define that person for the rest of his or her life. Most birth announcements also record the vital statistics of the date, time, weight, and length of the baby at birth. (Tip from an older mom: you think you will always remember these important numbers. Granted, you will never forget the date, but trust me—three children and many years later—those other numbers start blurring together. "How much did I weigh?" your teenager asks. "What exact time of day was I born?" Those questions might send you scrambling to remember.)

Birth announcements get pasted into baby books or displayed in picture frames. Our three are framed on a wall in a hallway. The first looks like a lawyer's professional announcement (since Daddy is a lawyer) announcing a new addition to the partnership of Kuykendall and Kuykendall. The second shows a picture of the older brother announcing his new baby sister's arrival. And the third is a Christmas card, announcing that our family is hanging up a new stocking this year.

For generations, birth announcements have served as a reminder of a family's celebration that says, "We're a FAMILY! We're celebrating. We hope you'll celebrate with us!"

Create Your Own Space

A year after the birth of our first child, we moved back to Colorado, where both sets of parents and two siblings lived. Lynn was getting out of the Navy, my father had just died, and I was pregnant with our second child. Coming back home seemed the logical choice because we wanted our children to grow up with grandparents and cousins and aunts and uncles nearby. But soon we realized that we faced a challenge all young families face at some point: how do we establish our own family within our larger family?

How do we create our own space? Our own boundaries? Our own family?

For some, this question pops up much earlier, even when planning the wedding. That's when you might discover that families can be complicated. And opinionated! So you find yourself trying to stand firm as you establish yourselves as an almost-family. I know one young man whose aunt and uncle decided they didn't like the woman he was engaged to marry. Their reasons were superficial, and for the first time in his life, he had to stand up to his older relatives and firmly say, "She is going to be my wife. I love and support her."

Some people don't feel like a family until they become parents. Having a child seems to validate their status as a family and gives them the confidence to create their own space and make their own choices based on their new priorities.

When we moved back to Colorado after five years of marriage, we brought a more mature kind of confidence. Now that we were parents, we felt like adults instead of kids who happened to be married. Before having children, we were like kids who still felt obligated to please our parents and guilty when we did not—not always because they made us feel that way but because we allowed ourselves to feel that way. We simply couldn't meet everyone's expectations. On visits, we never could stay long enough. We didn't call often enough. Or talk long enough when we did. But now that we had children, we had legitimate reasons to focus on different priorities. We could put our own family first.

When a new family starts growing within a family, everyone faces some adjustments, and everyone has to be willing to embrace change as we create our own space for our family to grow. In this way, a family is like a tapestry, a unique and colorful piece of fabric with many individual threads and patterns woven through it. As children grow up, they weave themselves farther and farther away from the original family pattern. They go out with their own friends on Friday night instead of joining the family for pizza. They miss the first family vacation. They move out and go off to college.

New threads are added as children marry and eventually bring their own children into the family tapestry. They begin to create their own space and weave their own unique family circle, which stretches and tugs at the fabric. Ultimately, of course, these new patterns add richness and texture to the family tapestry, but both the fabric and the threads need to be flexible enough to embrace all the growing and changing patterns.

Creating your own space means accepting your new role as an adult with influence and not letting guilt shape your choices—guilt that you heap on yourself or guilt heaped on by someone else. This guilt is most typically experienced during holidays. At Christmas we might load the kids in the car and spend the day traveling around to visit grandparents and cousins, because it's easier to drive all day and make them happy than to *not* drive and deal with all the guilt trips. Over time, patterns of response based on guilt can rip the fabric of a family apart.

God intends for families to create their own space, as described by the words used in many wedding ceremonies: "A man leaves his father and his mother and cleaves to his wife, and they become one flesh" (Gen. 2:24 RSV). No doubt the *leaving* part is easily understood, but *cleaving* sounds weird, like separating meat with a sharp knife. *Cleaving* can mean "separating," but here it also means "joining together," so *cleaving* in marriage means that you are separate but glued together. You can't be separated without wounding and damaging both people.

Honoring the *leaving and cleaving* process allows generations of families to remain part of a growing tapestry, while making room for new patterns to be woven into the fabric.

In spite of your best efforts, you're still bound to face some messy family issues as you create your own family space. Threads don't tie neatly, or they get knotted together too

---

"Call it a clan, call it a network, call it a tribe, call it a family. Whatever you call it, you need one."
~ Jane Howard

---

tightly. Many of those knots involve issues about your child. Here are a few common ones.

Delivery—who's invited? Take the issue of the delivery, for instance. By this time, you've already faced the issue of whether your family agrees with your decision to find out (or not find out) the sex of your unborn child. Now you have to decide who will be present at the delivery. Is this a private moment, with just you and your husband? How about your mom? And where does your mother-in-law fit in? The choices are yours, of course, but they might not make everyone else happy.

Then there's the issue of who comes to visit and when during the first few weeks after a child is born or adopted into a family. How do you choose and set the time limits for how long relatives stay without hurting someone's feelings? How do you divide the time between two sets of grandparents and possibly stepgrandparents? Keeping score can be complicated. Especially if you're not the one keeping score.

Naming the baby: How about the issue of naming your baby? If you choose to find out the sex of your baby before the birth, you have lots of time to announce to the world the names you're considering. Have you gotten any rolls of the eyes on the possibilities? Did your brother-in-law delight in telling you that Scot, your chosen name, will surely become Scotty-Potty or Snotty Scotty on the playground in first grade? Or that Stacey will become Spacey Stacey?

Parenting: How about issues with the way you are raising your child? Whether you nurse or not. How long you nurse. Whether you let your baby cry when you put him or her down. How strict you are about naptimes, or how picky you are about day care. The way you discipline. Or don't. Or whether your methods are more or less effective than those your parents used.

Unmet expectations: What about your own expectations of the way you'd like your parents to respond to your children? "I'd love to have the problem of overly involved parents, but my mom is underly involved," one mom said. "She's too busy, and that makes me both sad and mad."

Sibling rivalry—again: If you spend time with your extended family, you may run into some new feelings of competition. Your older brother obviously has the favored child. Or your sister has the spoiled child. After all, her child hit your child first. But her child is the youngest, so she got all the sympathy.

Doing Differently

All these issues and the responses they elicit can get pretty messy as you work at creating your own space and becoming your own family within a family. As I look back over my years of dealing with these issues, I wish I'd done some things differently along the way. I realize now that the way I responded to the issues I faced early in our family life formed a pattern in the way I continued to approach those issues. Such patterns are hard (but not impossible) to change.

Lighten Up

When I was a new mom, I sometimes created tensions simply because I wanted to clearly set us apart as our own family. I criticized unnecessarily. Or decided to do things differently only for the sake of being different. I wanted a sense of control, so we made rules we didn't need to make. "We will alternate Christmas every other year with our families!" Or, "We will stay home every year." The *every* part doesn't always work out or make room for unplanned circumstances. So we've created a rule that even we don't want to keep.

I also took too many things personally. For instance, my mother-in-law baked my husband cherry pies all the time (only because I didn't?). Or gave him pajamas every Christmas (only because I didn't?). I now know that kind of defensiveness said more about me than her. Besides, I see the adult mother-son relationship differently now that I have a son myself.

When a daughter gets married, if her relationship with her mother is good, she may still look to her mother for a kind of nurturing she doesn't get from her husband. After I got married, in spite of Lynn's best efforts, I still had some "I need my mom" kind of days. There were times when I didn't feel good and could count on her to say, "Oh honey, you need to stay in bed today." Even though both of us knew I couldn't possibly stay in bed, her words made me feel better. And needing my mom in that way also made her feel better.

However, when a son gets married, that kind of nurturing is transferred to the wife—as it should be—so his mother loses what used to be an important part of their relationship. It goes back to the biblical model of leaving and cleaving, but it's good to cut a mother-in-law some slack for the ways she might want to maintain a relationship with her son, especially when it doesn't interfere with the husband-wife relationship. The fact is, I didn't make cherry pies, so why not be grateful that she did? Besides, one of the best ways I can love my husband is to love his parents as best I can.

Communicate Clearly

When issues did arise in our families, I wish I'd learned to tell the truth—in love. Not in self-defense or anger. In love. In order to make an important relationship better. Too often

---

Family is . . .
The foundation on which we build our lives.

I stuffed my feelings and chose silence until a major blow-up happened. Other mothers admit the same response. "If I tell my sister that her remarks about my child make me mad, she'll tell me I am being overly sensitive." Or, "If I tell my mother-in-law that her comments about our Christmas plans make me feel guilty, she'll get irritated." So we say nothing, becoming pseudo peacemakers instead of real truth tellers. Though your efforts may feel risky, learning to lovingly tell the truth builds authentic relationships that allow a family to grow within family. You'll feel better, and eventually your family will feel better as well.

Here are a few guidelines for a lovingly honest conversation:

- Identify the real issue. Are your feelings hurt? Do you feel misunderstood? Ignored or overlooked? Do these feelings even fit this situation, or are they leftovers from another issue?
- Have the conversation face-to-face, if possible, as soon as possible.
- Affirm the relationship first. "I really care about you and our relationship, so I'd like to talk about something that might help our relationship grow."
- Use "I" messages about your feelings rather than accusing the other person. For instance, "I'm feeling hurt by something you said, which may be a misunderstanding, so can we talk about it?"
- Keep the issue between the two people involved. Avoid sharing unnecessarily with other family members.

Relationships Come First

Some things have changed since I was a young mom, but what matters most has not changed. Relationships matter, and God created us to be in relationship with others, starting with our families. They offer the closest circle of relationships that are intended for the support and encouragement of each other. So if you feel yourself getting tangled in tensions, stop and ask, "What matters most here? What will matter next week at this time, or next year at this time? How can I *do* what matters most right now?" Those questions help us sort out the important from the trivial, extend grace to each other, and keep growing authentic relationships as we continue to make adjustments to our changing roles in a family.

I can't resist this final story, since it illustrates how some things have changed since I was a mom with young children. That was before cell phones (gasp!) and pagers were connected to the human body. And before those indispensable baby monitors were invented. All these things are supposed to make your life easier, but they can also create some new (and amusing!) wrinkles in our family relationships.

Here's the story: A young couple took their six-month-old baby to visit his parents (therefore *her* in-laws). The night they arrived, the proud grandparents hosted a fancy dinner party in their honor. So, after showing off the baby, the parents tucked their precious little bundle into the Pack 'N Play in the upstairs bedroom where the three would be sleeping. They dutifully turned on the baby monitor and plugged the other monitor in the dining room, turning up the volume as they joined the dinner party. Just as dessert and coffee were being served, the young couple excused themselves, feigning fatigue and saying goodnight. Quietly they crawled into bed upstairs, whereupon they began to do what married couples do in bed. "Quite enthusiastically," as the young mom describes. It was not until much later that they realized they had not turned off the baby monitor on the nightstand next to them. At breakfast the next morning, they didn't dare ask how long it took for someone to turn off the baby monitor in the dining room during dessert at the dinner party.

Hmmm . . . maybe technology doesn't always make everything better. At least this couple was showing that their own relationship was still a top priority for them. And they did create a space for themselves.

In the first few years, you celebrate the creation of your family in ways that deepen its significance. You also create a space for your family, setting yourselves apart within your larger family. Maybe you have one child, maybe more, but in these first early years, you are shaping your own family in many lasting ways.

"We're a family!" you are announcing.

Now, what kind of family do you want to become?

Wonderings

---

1. "We're a FAMILY!" When did that realization hit you, and what did it mean to you?
2. Play the word-association game. Say the word *family* out loud. What other words come to mind? Write them down:

   _____

   _____

   _____

   Why did you choose those words?
3. Pregnancy and birth announcements are great ways to celebrate the news that a new baby is joining your family. What creative ways have you heard to celebrate this news? (For instance, a BABY photograph frame with the words "Photo due in February"; or framing the pregnancy test strip or sonogram picture.)
4. Look at the issues listed in this chapter: birth and coming home; baby's name; raising your child; unmet expectations; sibling jealousy. What issues do you face

in creating your own "family within a family"? How are you resolving these issues?

5. What do you want or need most from your extended family? Are you able to communicate that desire to them? Why or why not?

2

Family Dreams

*What Kind of Family
Do We Want to Be?*

Let's pretend.

You're sitting at the kitchen table, flipping through one of your favorite catalogs early one Saturday morning, sipping a toffee nut latte with extra whipped cream that was just delivered to your front door by Starbucks. Your two preschoolers are playing happily and quietly with each other in the next room. (I know, none of these circumstances seem real, but remember . . . we're playing "let's pretend!")

The phone rings, and a voice on the other end identifies herself as a reporter for the *New York Times*. She got your name from your best friend in high school who also works in New York City. The reporter is doing a front-page article on families. Of course your comments will remain anonymous if you wish, but here's what she wants to know: What are your dreams for your family? What kind of family do you want to become?

How would you answer?

Maybe you are momentarily stumped. Should you be funny, flip, or dead serious? You probe around your brain for an answer. How about a family that looks like the one in your favorite TV sitcom? A family that is real and honest, but still loving, in their own unique way. Sure they have problems, especially with their extended family, but they work all those out in thirty-minute time frames. And they are so funny!

Or how about a quieter, more deeply spiritual family? A Billy Graham family where you may deal with some normal rebellion with your kids, but they grow up to see the light and serve the Lord in powerful ways.

Then again, maybe you don't even know where to start. So you beg off as nonchalantly as you can and hang up. You turn from the phone and . . . poof! The pretend game is over! Reality returns. Your latte is replaced by a cup of lukewarm tea. Your children are running through the kitchen, screaming, and shooting each other with pretend guns (which you hate). The dog chases after them, barking loudly. Suddenly you have an answer to the pretend question. What you dream about is a family where everyone gets along . . . quietly. A family that manages the chaos.

What Are Your Dreams?

Do you have dreams for your family? Are you intentionally aiming for some goals? Have you thought about your family's purpose—or defined the kind of family you want to be ten years from now? If you don't have a quick answer, you're normal. When caring for young children, who has energy for anything more than surviving the demands of the moment: getting through to the pediatrician before the neighborhood pharmacy closes; finding shoes to fit all the growing feet; putting mac 'n' cheese on the table and getting all the kids in bed so you can go to bed? Then your dream is about being in bed long enough to be able to dream!

Who has time to dream about the future when dealing with the present is so consuming?

As I look back, I realize I dreamed more about the family I wanted before I had a family of my own. As a teenager, I used to watch other families and fantasize about the ones I might want to live with because they seemed to have more fun than my own. After Lynn and I got married, we began watching families because we knew we'd start our own someday and dreaming was exciting during those first few years of marriage. When we visited families with young children, I watched how the parents solved cranky-kid problems with humor. I checked out the stuff on their refrigerator door and the family photos on display around the house. What were they doing in those pictures? How did they talk to each other? What were their secrets to getting along well together?

Then we had three children in five years, and we felt way too distracted by today to think much about tomorrow. And nobody from the *New York Times* ever called and asked me to put my dreams into words. Yet now when I look back on those years, I realize that we did have some dreams that evolved as we began raising our family.

Dreams are important. Dreams are visions for what we do not yet have, so they give us something to aim for in the future. A dream serves as that bright North Star that beckons and guides us through our days and nights. Reaching for that star keeps us heading in the right direction. When we get off track (which we will!), it gives us something to come back to. It's been said, "We dream, therefore we become." We also know that if we aim for nothing, we're bound to hit it!

Our children need us to dream and have goals. When they are young, they are totally dependent upon us for guidance. They don't yet know how fallible we are. In their eyes, we rule! They need us to care about our purpose as a family. They need us to have a vision of where we're headed and a plan for how we're going to get there. They need us to lead them.

Besides, strong families don't just happen. They happen "on purpose."

What are your dreams for your family?

Your answer matters, and coming up with it might be easier than you think. It starts with looking back at the family you had, looking around at the family you have, and then looking forward to the family you want to become. This process gives us perspective as we see how yesterday fits into today and helps us to shape tomorrow. It helps us define our purpose for our family.

Looking Back: The Family You Had

What kind of family did you grow up in? You are still part of that family, and your childhood experiences influence the family you are creating today, just as your parents' lives were shaped by their parents' lives. No wonder some of those family patterns or behaviors are repeated in families for generations. Automatically—without awareness.

Sometimes we feel guilty about looking back and evaluating our childhood because it seems dishonoring to our parents, who, in most cases, did the best they could. In other cases, we slip all too easily into the role of critic and miss the good that was there, though maybe a few layers deep.

Objectively evaluating the ways we grew up is part of the process of growing up. We look back not as critics but as parents who want to understand how our own childhood experiences affect who we are and how we interact with our families today. We pick out the good parts in order to pass them on, and we identify the not-so-good parts in order to process through them and be intentional about not passing them on.

And guess what? Our children will do the same thing. My grown children today will mention some seemingly small moment that seared itself into their impressionable souls decades ago . . . a moment when I didn't listen well or understand their feelings or love them the way they wanted to be loved. I used to feel guilty and defensive about their

---

> **"Know where you are headed,**
> **and you will stay on solid ground."**
> **~ Proverbs 4:26 CEV**

---

memories of times I failed them. After all, I always feared I'd ruin them by unknowingly doing things that would put them into therapy and keep them from getting into the colleges of their choice.

But I've gotten a bit less melodramatic about their recollections now. They are doing exactly what I have done in reviewing my own growing-up years. Looking back and evaluating is normal, and the more I can normalize my responses—instead of getting all defensive—the more we can laugh together at all these family faux pas. (And I can't wait for their children to grow up and do the same thing!)

I have mostly good memories of my childhood. I was born on the cutting edge of the baby-boomer generation. I grew up in the fifties, in a family of six with two younger brothers and an older sister. Our family lived the norm at that time when there was a clear division of duties: moms took care of the children and dads went to work. My father wasn't present at any of our births and worked long hours as an advertising executive. My mother was a freelance writer who also dabbled in real-estate and remodeling projects, all home based.

My family lived on a hillside in the country near Boulder, Colorado, with all sorts of animals, including horses, cats, dogs, rabbits, and even a couple of lambs, called Lamb Chops and Lamb Stew. My mother had grown up in New York City as an only child after her older sister died at age three, an experience her own mother never fully recovered from. As a lonely child, my mother vowed that she would grow up to live in the country and have lots of animals and at least four children, which she did, in spite of her doctor's advice to terminate her fourth pregnancy because of a threat to her own life.

My parents both had a strong sense of family loyalty, and spending time together was a high priority, which sometimes demanded my mother's creativity. When we were young, she bought a large farm truck that she tried to transform into one of the world's first RVs (but not nearly so nice!). She tied a huge piece of canvas over the truck's open bed, kind of like a covered wagon, and put in a stove and refrigerator, a chest of drawers, and a long table.

Here's the part I have more trouble believing now than I did then. The table folded down and became a barrier to the furnishings, so she could load our three horses into this RV-truck, and off we'd all go to the mountains, like gypsies, for long summer weekends. After unloading the horses and sweeping out the yuck in the truck, we slept in it at night. During the days, we went on long trail rides where we learned some memorable family rules, like, "No complaining about being tired, hungry, or thirsty. Or smelling like a horse."

We spent winters riding the school bus back and forth to a country school where I once took my rambunctious four-year-old brother for show-and-tell, which was a disaster because I couldn't control him and we made a horrible scene. That night (and many times afterward) my mother told me and my little brother, "You can argue all you want behind closed doors, but when you go out into the world, you stick together and get along." Her words must have sunk in eventually, because I grew up knowing there was lots we did in life (and lots we didn't do) "because we're family." But family loyalty also caused me to stuff some of my more unhappy memories.

My father was a stern Dutchman with a temper that sometimes frightened me. I have one incredibly vivid memory of something that happened when I was probably about seven or eight. My father was on his way out the front door when I opened the refrigerator door. Suddenly all the glass milk bottles came tumbling out, crashing to the floor, splattering milk and shattered glass all over the kitchen. I was horrified at the sight and even more horrified by my father's anger as he came running back into the house to punish me for something I didn't do.

Those memories—good or bad—shape the way I influence our family today and give me words for the dreams I continue to have for the family we are still becoming. Family is a priority. Animals enrich our lives. Rolling with the punches and persevering is more important than whining and complaining. Creativity matters. Angry outbursts can frighten others, and physical punishment can be misused. Also, a mother's childhood vows and dreams can shape her family's lives.

Most of us have a combination of good and some not-so-good memories of our childhood. No family is perfect, and if we think ours was, we're apt to be masking an objective look at issues that might have been difficult. On the other hand, we sometimes overcriticize our parents, when in reality most of them did better than we give them credit for.

As for the normal disappointments and past hurts, we have some choices. To accept them, grieve them, forgive and let go of them, and move on. Or wallow in them and blame our current problems or unhappiness on them, letting them fill us with bitterness. We can't change our past circumstances, and

---

Family is . . .
The place you call home.

---

we can't change our family members, but we can change our responses to those memories. We can create a vision for our future in spite of our past. Sometimes we need help in that process, which is available through capable, recommended counselors.

"I didn't have much healthy love from my mother, which left me with lots of holes," one mom remembers. "But I've learned that I can fill some of those holes by giving my children what I didn't have. I'm getting it as I give it."

"I ate way too much mac 'n' cheese alone in front of the television," another said. "What I knew is that I didn't want to grow up and have a family like that."

As we deal with the realities of our "looking back" process, we can be comforted in knowing that God understands any dysfunctions in our families. In fact, the whole Bible is the story of a dysfunctional family. It is the story about how we as God's children go our own way and do our own thing, and how God forgives us and brings us back into relationship with himself through Jesus. Our past does not have to dictate our future, and we can unlearn harmful habits rather than pass them on in our own families. As for the hurts, we can find healing as we invest ourselves in our families.

In the movie *My Big Fat Greek Wedding*, Toula's brother, Nick, encourages Toula not to be overwhelmed by their big, noisy, nosy family. "Don't let your past dictate who you are," he tells her, "but let it be a part of who you become."

So here's a question: *as you look back at your own family upbringing, in what ways do you want your family to be the same, and in what ways do you want your family to be different?*

Looking Around: The Family You Have

When dreaming about the family you want to become in the future, you also have to look at the family you are today, including the size of your family, ages of your children, cultural family backgrounds, physical or emotional limitations, geographical location, and working situations, to name just a few of the circumstances that influence the dreams you may have for your family.

A couple of principles guide us here. The first is to *accept where we are*—because we start from where we are—in the present. We sometimes get so stuck in the past or wrapped up in the anticipation of the future that we can't focus on the present. I know a mom who was so fixated on her past with an emotionally uninvolved mother that she could hardly assess the present until she got help from a counselor. Many parents worry about the future and the influences of the big bad world on our families. We try to figure out ways to control that future rather than seize the moments of today to equip our children to become adults who will be able to cope in that world today and tomorrow.

Another principle is to *accept who we are*. Each family has some unique circumstances—both joys and challenges—that are an important part of who we are as a family. The mom who was dealing with regrets about her emotionally uninvolved mother had to accept the fact that her mom was also going to be an emotionally uninvolved grandmother and then shape her dreams for her family around that reality. Another family with two adopted children from China dedicated themselves to incorporating elements of Chinese culture into their family traditions and family future.

Our son, Derek, was diagnosed diabetic at age nine. From then on, our family dealt with the reality of living with diabetes, including daily insulin shots, blood tests, the constant critical balance of food and exercise, and the inevitable frightening reactions when he got out of balance. In dreaming about our future as a family and Derek's future as an individual, we vowed not to let diabetes limit his choices, but we still had to accept the reality and daily responsibility of living with it.

A single mom said she had to accept the brokenness of her family and find comfort in knowing that God understands our brokenness and uses even our difficult circumstances to grow us into the people he wants us to become.

Every family faces similar reality checks as they recognize who they are and the unique joys and challenges they live with. So here's another question: *what is unique about your family today, and how does that shape your dreams for the future?*

Looking Forward: The Family You Want to Become

You've looked back at the family in which you grew up, identifying the ways you do or don't want your family today to be like your original family. You've considered the unique qualities and circumstances of your family now and how that reality shapes your dreams for the future.

So where do we go from here?

We look ahead to the future by dreaming about the kind of family we want to become and putting words to those dreams. We then hold those words out in front of us like the North Star that shines and beckons us as we seek to shine in the same way and become the family we want to be.

Let's start dreaming.

A good way to get started is to think about the end result, or the way you hope your family will be when your kids are all grown up and you are adults together. Here are a couple of questions to get you warmed up. What kind of husband or father do you want your son to become? Or what kind of college freshman do you hope your daughter will become? We live in a college town where local newspaper articles give us frequent glimpses into the lives of kids living away from home, probably for the first time. Some drink too much. Some try to climb sheer canyon walls without proper equipment. One recently defended her faith in a freshman science class. Some study; some don't. What do you hope a newspaper reporter will write about your child as a college freshman?

Look around. Watch other families that you admire, families who get along well. Think of the words that describe that family and therefore the family you want to become. Or the words that describe the family you don't want to become.

My husband is an attorney, doing mostly wills and estates, so he meets regularly with families to talk about what will happen to their investments and possessions after they die. All too often, he deals with parents and children or siblings who haven't spoken to each other for years. The original rift usually started long ago, and everybody let it fester and grow instead of working it out and moving on. Now they avoid each other at all costs. They don't attend the same family weddings or reunions. They never communicate at holidays. So when one faces the emotional challenge of dealing with end-of-life details, the rift becomes painfully obvious.

I don't want to be like that family.

Here are some of our North Star words that describe our dreams. In spite of all the distractions of raising young children, these are the qualities we aimed for as our children were growing up. One is love. I've wanted ours to be a loving family that cares enough to face problems and deal with them; a family that doesn't let grudges grow but does

---

"You are the poem I dreamed of writing ...
the masterpiece I longed to paint.
You are the shining star I reached for."
~ Author unknown

---

encourage each other to grow and change. The fact is, we'll probably spend twice as many years as adults together with our children as we do actively parenting them. They may live with us for about eighteen years, but God willing, we'll be in relationship with them for at least twice that many years after they leave home. So I want to build the kind of family relationships that are based on love that endures and grows. I want a family who is loyal and committed and kind to each other.

I don't want to be a sarcastic family, where humor is based on constant, hurtful put-downs. I don't want to be a yelling family or an apathetic family who doesn't care much about spending time together.

I want to be a family that has fun together, but I want us to be about more than having fun and getting along. More than doing a bunch of things I'm proud to report in our annual Christmas letter. More than having good health. I want to be the kind of family who knows how to live when the health isn't so good. Or the accomplishments aren't so successful, or the circumstances aren't so happy. I want us to stand for something beyond ourselves and beyond today.

I want us to reflect the trust we have in God and shine like that bright North Star, passing hope on to others who live in a darker place.

Those are some of the words that describe my dreams. If you were to pick the most important ones out of the sentences above, you would find these: love, fun, loyalty, growth, and faith. These also happen to be the ones I've heard most often from other parents when I ask them to describe their dreams for their families. In this book, each one represents one of the five points on that shining North Star, as we seek to shine like a star in the universe.

Though we're bound to already have some of these qualities in our families, we need all five together. *Love* meets our greatest needs; *fun* makes us want to be together; *loyalty* and commitment connect us together; *growth* keeps us healthy; and *faith* gives us hope and lights our way.

These qualities brighten and illuminate each other. Love without fun is dull and boring. Growth without faith is shallow and dead-end. Love and loyalty deepen each other. As one mom pointed out, "My husband was raised in a strong, loyal family, but without much love. We hit a major bump in our marriage when our children were young. Lots of little things. I remember looking at him one day, thinking he would probably never divorce me, because his sense of loyalty was so strong, but the thought of a forever marriage that was loveless was terrifying. I didn't want us to be stuck in loyalty that was loveless."

Because of their faith and commitment to grow, this couple sought counseling and worked through their differences. Today they are in a much different place as a family.

God created families as a gift of relationships with great potential to grow. He puts dreams in our hearts to give us a vision and desire for that potential. He makes us, the adults, the leaders in our families and equips us to lead toward our goals. Toward a bright and shining future as a five-star family.

Love, fun, loyalty, growth, and faith . . . do these words describe your dreams for your family?

Wonderings

1. In view of the way you grew up, name three ways you want your family to be the same:

   _____

   _____

   _____

   Name three ways you want to be different:

   _____

   _____

   _____

2. What is unique about your family? How does your uniqueness shape your dreams for your family's future?

3. What are the dreams you have for your family? What words describe those dreams? Here are some questions to get you thinking:

   If you have more than one child, what words describe the relationships you hope your children will have with each other?

   What words describe the way you hope your family would respond to winning the lottery? An unexpected death in your family? An invitation to attend a family reunion? Fears about terrorists?

Dream Catchers

You can't maintain your dreams alone. You need some "Dream Catchers," people who help you hold and remain committed to your dreams for your family. Here are some suggestions:

Spouse: If you are married, your first helpmate in realizing your family dreams is your spouse. Dream together. Read the questions in this section together. Talk to each other about your childhood family experiences and the ways you want your family to be different or the same. Observe other families and together discuss the qualities you admire. If you're stuck, discuss the kind of family you don't want to be, and then choose the opposites of those words. They describe your dreams together.

Mentors: A mentor is usually an older person or couple who is a bit further down the road than you are in this family journey. A mentor can help you focus on the bigger picture, which is sometimes hard to see in the pressure of the present. You get a mentor simply by asking. Look around for a family growing in the direction you want your family to grow. Then ask that person or couple if they might meet with you. Be specific about your request. You might say, "Would you be willing to meet regularly (once a week or month) until January (define a time to at least reevaluate the relationship) to talk about family goals?" Be specific about whether you want informal question-and-answer conversation or whether you'd like to go through a book together.

Small Groups: Gathering regularly with other moms or couples can normalize your challenges. As you share your experiences, you will realize that you are not alone. You can talk together about ways to model the purposes you identify as important to your family. A word of caution, however: we all get passionate about our opinions, especially when it comes to parenting. So you're bound to meet people who think you should agree with their opinions. If you don't, they assume you must be wrong (because that makes them right). Small groups should offer safe places to express opinions, in spite of your differences. Many moms of young children find this kind of safe, accepting environment in a MOPS (Mothers of Preschoolers) group.

Church Family: Being part of a church family helps you raise your family. Our pastor and church friends gave us much-needed guidance and prayer support through the years. We attended church classes where we learned about family goals and relationships. We shared books and participated in lively discussion groups. We learned to distinguish between the kind of fear-based teaching that assumes the safest way to raise our families is to close ranks around them and protect them from the world—and the teaching that encourages us to enter into our world in order to bring the light of hope to others.

How do you hope your family responds to the needs of people in the larger world around you? A friend's needs? Your neighbor's needs? A hungry child in another country? How will you help them learn the responses you hope for?

4. Write some of your dream words for your family in the center of this star so you can hold those words before you as you continue to think about the five-star qualities.

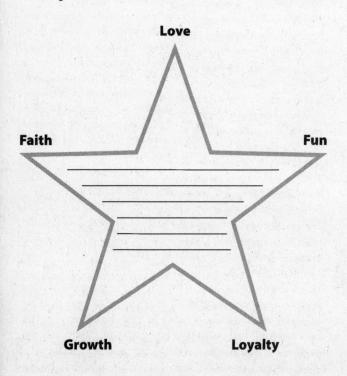

52

3

Family Surprises

Wow! Children Bring Us "Gifts"!

Allow me to push the pause button momentarily.

Before we look at the five-star qualities of love, fun, loyalty, growth, and faith, let me tell you about something that has surprised me—and profoundly shaped my understanding of how families grow from good to great!

It's about the gifts that children bring to a family. Especially the gift of mutual growth. Before I became a mother, I assumed that my main responsibility would be to love our children and grow them up. How wrong I was! I now see that my responsibility is also to allow them to grow me down. Down into childlikeness. Down into humility and wonder. Down into authenticity. Down into all the godlike qualities God never intends us to grow out of ... no matter how old we are.

When we adults open ourselves up to fully receive these gifts from our children, we catch glimpses of the one who gives us our children.

Our children are a gift from God. And they bring gifts that remind us of the gift-giver.

Gifts have a way of doing that, don't they?

I'm thinking of the gift Lynn gave me on my birthday recently. Our family gathered for a Sunday brunch celebration, which included unwrapping some presents. From our children, I received perfume (I love it!), a hair dryer (I needed it!), and some makeup (I needed that even more!). Next I opened Lynn's gift, a big box but very light. Lynn is a good gift-giver but likes my specific requests to help him in his quest. This year, he didn't even ask, so I knew this gift would be a surprise.

It was! Inside the box was a pair of goofy-looking rubber shoes called Crocs that are very "in" now in Colorado, especially with the younger, hip athletic types. They are so ugly that they're fashionable. They aren't exactly what I expected, but I love that my pragmatic lawyer husband went to a specialty store and purchased these whimsical shoes for me. All his own idea. Of course I love these shoes now, and every time I wear them, I think of Lynn.

The gift reminds me of the giver.

Children do the same. They are gifts that remind us of the giver.

Children Are a Gift from God

Most likely, when a child comes into your family through birth or adoption, you have a moment when you recognize this child as a gift from God. Maybe the gift doesn't look or act exactly as you expected. Maybe you waited longer than you wanted for this gift. Or maybe the gift came too early and surprised you. But there is a moment—for most of us—that we realize that a birth mother or birth father has little to do with the incredible, intricate creation of a heart and brain and fingernails and eyelashes and kneecaps. I labored and delivered three children, and though I still have vivid memories of the laboring, I also remember feeling utterly awed that God allowed me to participate in the miracle of his creation.

"Children are . . . a gift from the LORD" (Ps. 127:3 CEV), and surely the God of creation intends that as we receive these gifts, we allow the wonder of their beings to enter into all the hardened, controlling, numbed-down, scabbed-over parts of our hearts—and remind us of him.

When we first receive these gifts, we have no idea that we will be unwrapping them for the rest of our lives, discovering who they are while allowing them to continually help us discover who we are. While we are trying to make them into the people we think they should be, we hardly recognize how God is using them to make us into the people he created us to be.

I'm convinced that God intends this mutual growth process. In fact, surrendering to this process—rather than resisting it—helps us reach our greatest potential as a family. Do you know what "resisting it" looks like? It means assuming that as parents, we are in control. Surrendering means recognizing that ultimately God is in control and trusting that control, which allows each of us to be shaped by him for his purposes, not ours.

The surprises of this process are tucked into our everyday experiences, when we're brushing our teeth or buckling up and riding in the car or saying bedtime prayers.

For sure, children are gifts that keep on giving.

Children Bring Gifts from God

Let's consider some of the transforming gifts children bring us. As we receive these gifts and acknowledge where they come from, we see the character of God.

Gift of Do-Overs

I've often heard that you don't get "do-overs" in life.
I disagree.

God gives us a huge do-over when he gifts us with children. When a child comes into our lives, we get a second chance at childhood, a second chance to read *Winnie-the-Pooh* and pick up on the messages we might not have understood the first time. We get a second chance to fill in the holes left over from our own childhood as we choose to do things differently this time around. As a friend said, "Mothering my child gives me some control over a part of my life in which I had no control when I was growing up." We have the opportunity to be surprised again by the things of childhood that we might have missed or forgotten.

Children give us do-overs, a gift that reminds us of the God who gives us second chances.

Gift of Wonder

We are born with an amazing capacity for wonder, a gift from the God of wonder who creates us in his image. This wonder inspires our awe for God—and all that he creates. Yet as we grow up, we go through a numbing-down process and experience this awe less and less. A teenager is rarely wowed by a moo from a cow. Or a bunch of ants busily constructing their underground community. Or a hawk soaring in the sky. But as we watch a child respond to these sights and sounds, we remember the wonder.

A child's wonder is contagious. One mom said that her daughters have helped her rediscover the world. "I will never again take for granted a car wash, swing set, or rainbow. My four-year-old wants her daddy to put a ladder up high to the rainbow so she can climb up and ride that rainbow through the sky. What a beautiful thought!"

Wonder-filled children gift us with their playful imagination. They infuse us with make-believe friends and mixed-up word choices and joyful anticipation about what might happen to a simple avocado seed, held in place by toothpicks in a paper cup filled with water.

We delight in taking children to a zoo or a parade or a children's museum because their excitement overflows and spills out all over us. When they ask "why?" we realize all we've taken for granted, and we wonder "why?" right along with them. Why do stars shine? Why do only your bottom teeth move when you chew? Why do we hear an echo in this mountain canyon? We are wonder-filled once again at God's creation.

Wonder is defined as spontaneous praise. The involuntary "Wows!" But how empty that praise becomes if we can't direct it somewhere. What if we felt awed by a spectacular sunset but didn't know who to thank?

A child's gift of wonder directs our praise to the God of wonder.

Gift of Humility

In growing up, we learn to be self-sufficient and independent. We learn to cover up what we don't know and resist asking for help because we don't want to look like we're not strong enough. Or smart enough. Children give us the gift of their honest, vulnerable dependency that helps us grow down and realize we can admit our need for help too. God doesn't intend for us to do life alone. Or mothering alone. We don't have all the answers. We get incredibly sleep deprived. Sometimes we're going to lose it with our kids.

Children reveal us to ourselves. They reveal our needs for patience. HELP! Wisdom. Kindness. Forgiveness. When we recognize our needs, we receive the holy opportunity to recognize our utter and desperate dependence on others and on God who meets our greatest needs.

Before I had children, I imagined that mothering would bring out the best in me. I looked back at my original family

---

Family means . . .

Being who you are and getting away with it.

---

and clearly knew what I did and did not want to pass on in my mothering. One thing I vowed I would not pass on was some of the language my parents sometimes used. Like when my mom really lost it with us kids, she'd blurt out "D--- you!" Those words frightened me as a child, and I vowed I'd never use that kind of language with my own children.

But I remember a day when I'd been up half the night with Kendall, our new baby, and my jeans still felt too tight, and five-year-old Derek and four-year-old Lindsay were picking on each other, and I'd totally run out of patience with their demands and "Mommy this . . ." and "Mommy that . . ." So I was trying to ignore them. In frustration, Lindsay gritted her teeth and grabbed my hand to get my attention, squeezing my little finger against the prongs of my wedding ring, hard! It hurt something fierce. . . .

"D--- you!" I blurted out—and then froze, looking at those words—hanging there in midair. They had come from a place that I didn't know existed inside me. And I cringed with guilt and shame as I searched the eyes of my child and feared that I was turning into the kind of mom I never wanted to be.

My children have revealed that mothering doesn't always bring out the best; it can also bring out the worst in me, and I have an ongoing need for forgiveness from the one who understands my guilt and shame. This gift reminds me of my own dependence and neediness, which turns me to the giver, who gives me hope in my not-yet-done-ness.

Gift of Childlike Faith

Children believe. They trust wholeheartedly. Jesus used children as visual aids when he wanted others to understand matters of faith. He called a child to him and said, "I tell you the truth, unless you change and become like little children, you will never enter the kingdom of heaven" (Matt. 18:3).

Children model faith and trust in those they love. They sing, "Jesus loves me this I know," and they believe the words. At MOPS, we got a letter from a mother recently. Her four-year-old was part of the MOPPETS program.

"Our son kept bringing home papers from MOPPETS, where he is learning about Jesus. My husband was moved to tears as he listened to his son say bedtime prayers. 'If he can learn that and believe it, maybe I can too,' he said. Now we're all going back to church."

They allowed a little child to lead them. They received a gift of childlike faith that reminded them of the giver. Maybe, in time, that family will remind others of the giver.

Gift of Growing Better

Today, as I look back on my years of mothering, I can clearly see how my children have made me better. They have home-schooled me in some of life's most profound lessons. They've given me glimpses of God's unconditional love. Love that is not earned because of what you do, but because of who you are.

Before my first child was born, he kicked me so hard, I thought I might burst. He sat on my bladder, which kept me close to a bathroom. When he made his grand entrance into the world, all eight-and-a-half pounds of him, he caused me great pain. Then he kept me up at night and pooped in his pants and spit up all over me. He did nothing to earn my love, and yet as I rocked him to sleep sometimes, I thought I might burst with sheer delight and love for him. And I got a glimpse of God's love for me.

My children have softened my edges. Before they came into our family, my opinions were filled with *always* and *never*. "My children will *always* do what I say; *never* whine for cookies all the way through the grocery store; *never* appear in public with green stuff coming out of their noses. . . ." Three children and many years later, I have lots fewer *always* and *nevers* in my life.

My children have widened my love. I not only love them, I love *all* children. I buy Girl Scout cookies from every child who knocks on our door, and I can't read the newspaper or listen to the news without aching for any child in need.

My children have made me more honest and real: I can't get away with stretching the truth about who I am and who I am not. Ever since they started talking, my children have been my accountability partners. They repeat what I say (even when I wish they wouldn't), and they tell me the truth—about myself!

I asked other moms how their children have made them better and was surprised how quickly they recognized the ways and responded with their own answers. One mom admitted she used to be a "trucker mouth" who hung out "with all sorts." She was always in a hurry because she had places to go and money to make. Then she had kids.

"Now I watch what I say and take my time to enjoy the simple things in life. I get a second chance to be a kid, play games, go to kid movies, play on the jungle gym. How many

How My Children Make Me Better . . .

- I now know what "love at first sight" means.

- My children have given me a picture of God's love for me.

- My girls make me more creative.

- My kids help me see my husband through different eyes. I remember he's *my* hero too.

- My children teach me about forgiveness as they fight and hug each other, almost at the same time. Instead of getting angry, they laugh at themselves and each other.

- My children keep me grounded. "Would Jesus have done that?" I asked my son in anger the other day. "Well, gee Mom, Jesus was perfect!" I try to remember that when I am being too hard on them—or myself.

- My child helps me live in the moment. Before, I rarely fully appreciated what I had at the time. Now I think, "No minute in my life is going to be better than this one right now, because my life is so filled with love."

- My children make me laugh.

- My son helps me be accountable. I often think: do I want him doing the same thing I'm doing, like pigging out on junk food? The answer is no!

- My daughter has taught me about a relationship with Jesus by the way she shares everything with him in prayer and asks him questions and asks questions about him.

- My children make me want to better myself for their sake.

people get to tuck their guardian angels into bed at night? I can. They have guided me to be a better person. I am not perfect and I do not know all the answers, but they are my teachers and I am a fast learner."

Another mom claims her daughter has made her less self-conscious. "Before she was born, I never would have tried on hats in a department store or danced silly dances just to make myself feel better. Now my daughter and I try on silly hats in department stores and even put on skits while wearing them. One of our favorite things to do at home is turn up the music and dance to our hearts' content."

Still another mom describes how being the mom of a special-needs child has taught her to slow down "because my world runs at a different pace. I've learned to stop competing in the 'my child can . . .' contests because my child's accomplishments are slower in coming, which makes them all the more special. I need to let God work with and through my child as he will. I need to trust him. And I've learned that I need others. I need speech therapists, physical therapists, teachers, physicians, and so on to help me help my child. And I need family, ministers, support groups, and friends to lean on and share concerns and joys. I have to share my child and myself."

Let a Child Lead You

The best way to fully receive the gifts God gives us through our children is to simply watch a child. I recently held our two-year-old granddaughter as she discovered the wonder of snow. Wide-eyed, she looked up into the falling flakes. Feeling their cold softness on her face. Examining a single intricate flake on her red parka. Wow!

Remember how you felt doing something for the first time? Experience that wonder again as you watch your child do something for the first time. Observe the moon through a telescope. Ride the Ferris wheel or merry-go-round at an amusement park. Pet a baby lamb. Watch fireworks.

See what a child sees. I remember feeling totally empty and out of creativity one day as I worked at my computer. So I put on my running shoes and headed out the door, hoping the fresh air and exercise would stimulate some endorphins (those feel-good chemicals released in our bodies when we get physical exercise). Instead, my then-five-year-old nephew, who lives next door, decided to join me. So much for the endorphins. I sighed silently as my pace was slowed to a snail crawl. We spent the next half hour turning over rocks and talking about beetles and slugs. But when I returned to my task at the computer, I realized that my time with a child had rejuiced some of the parched places within me.

Play simple "I wonder" games with a child, taking turns wondering:

I wonder . . . how spiders make webs.

I wonder . . . how the world would be if children were the bosses.

I wonder . . . what if we never felt afraid of anything?

I wonder . . . why wind blows.

Learn from a child's honesty. We assume that because we're grown-up, we have most of the answers. But children remind us that we don't. Dare to admit what you don't know. Or that you made a mistake.

When making a choice, listen to your children. Ponder their possibilities. Let them lead.

Simplify and slow the pace. We experience such pressure to grow our children and ourselves. We keep up a breakneck pace in our families, fearing we will miss out on something or our children will be left behind in the race for . . . what? What we really miss out on is the simplicity that allows us to fully appreciate the gifts that children bring us in this fleeting season of our lives.

Children are a gift from God. They are his gift bearers, bringing gifts that reveal our needs and meet our needs. When we fully receive these gifts, we open ourselves to the kind of mutual growth God intends in our families. And we approach these five-star qualities with a passion for possibilities.

Let's grow up and down together.

Wonderings

1. "Gifts remind us of the giver." Think of a memorable gift you've received. Maybe on your last birthday or Christmas. Maybe a gift you got as a child. How does the gift remind you of the giver?

2. If you could be a kid for a day, what would you do? (My answer: I'd run around all day in a bathing suit and not worry about what I looked like!)

3. Jesus tells us to "change and become like little children" (Matt. 18:3). What does that mean to you? Name three ways you can change and become like a child.

   _____

   _____

   _____

4. Need to ignite your wonder?

   Watch your child, and name three ways your child expresses wonder.

   Do something differently in your routine today. Drive a different way home. Find something new on your old route. Brush your teeth with the opposite hand.

   Grow down by playing hide-and-seek with your children. Play the same game with God today. Keep seeking him in hidden places all day long.

5. Find yourself a quiet time and place to look for wonder this week. Your backyard. A chair by a window. A neighborhood park. Take a paper and pencil and copy this verse: "Surely the LORD is in this place, and I was not aware of it" (Gen. 28:16). What ways are you aware of his presence in this place?

What Matters Most

Aiming for Five-Star Qualities

4

Love

Love Meets Our Greatest Needs

What matters most in your family?

That's a no-brainer for most of us. It's love.

From the Bible to our favorite songs to the message of the classic children's book *The Velveteen Rabbit*, we learn that love matters most in our relationships.

"Love one another," the Bible tells us.

"All we need is love," the song goes.

Love makes you real, the Skin Horse assures the Velveteen Rabbit.

With love, we thrive. Without it, we can die. And when we reach the end of our lives, we won't care about what we've accomplished; we'll care about how well we've loved and been loved by those closest to us.

No wonder a study by Columbia University and the National Institutes of Health showed that Americans want to experience loving family relationships more than any other personal experience (even way ahead of "satisfying sexual relations"!). No wonder we put love first in the five-star qualities.

We all want love-filled families because love meets our greatest needs for security and significance. God created us with these needs. Then, because he is both creator and provider, he created the family circle of relationships where these needs are intended to be met in an ongoing cycle of receiving and giving love to each other.

I've created my own simple picture of how this works.

We're all born with a deep hole of longing in our hearts. An empty place that creates a yearning to be loved. Experts confirm this reality, telling us that babies are born with no internal source of love. They arrive in this world totally dependent upon an external source of love to meet their needs for security (am I safe?) and significance (do I matter?). That love helps shape the baby's brain and intellect. That's why a mother's tender touch is so critically important in the first few months of an infant's life.

As a mother cares for her child, she pours her love into her baby's heart. Sometimes spoonful by teensy teaspoonful (like early on a sleep-deprived morning, when she is nursing the baby while trying to put cereal in bowls for her two older, more demanding preschoolers). Other times she pours her love in by the bucketsful (like on a quiet afternoon while she cuddles with her baby on the couch, uninterrupted). Regardless, these experiences of love begin to fill the baby's heart with loving memories, from which her child will draw strength for the rest of his or her life. Confidence to form loving relationships with others. Comfort when feeling lonely, afraid, or disappointed. This reservoir of memories also connects a child to the people who will offer continuing resources of love in a lifetime.

I confess that when our kids were young, descriptions like that made me cringe because I worried about all those times I wasn't so loving. Or patient or consistent. But I'm older now, and so are our kids, and this is what I know for sure about the family-circle cycle of love. Families are resilient. And kids respond more to patterns of love than individual incidents.

Sometimes we pour our love in. Other times, in what I called my "bad mommy moments," a bit leaks out of the reservoir. Those are the times when we're impatient or too busy to listen or we break a promise or just plain lose it with a child. But at the end of a week or month or year, there's still plenty left in their reservoirs for them to draw upon and know that they are loved. The principle is this: more love goes in than leaks out.

We can take heart knowing that through our everyday gestures and routines we are filling them up with experiences of love that will nurture and sustain them and remind them of what matters most in life. And even if they start growing in a different direction, as teenagers often do for a time, that reservoir remains. It is a permanent part of who they are, and it continues to hold the memories of love deposited there when they were young. It readily offers up the resources of strength and comfort when they choose to draw from it again.

In the midst of giving this love to our children, we also receive a wondrous kind of love that continually surprises us. It's another one of those gifts that children bring, as described in the last chapter about family surprises. In loving a child, we experience a love that seeps into the hidden nooks and crannies of our own hearts, filling up empty spaces that we didn't even know we had. In the beginning, it's an almost indescribable kind of love that you can't explain to people who have not had children.

I was especially surprised by this love, and I can describe it better now because I'm watching my own children experience it with their babies. Caring for a totally dependent infant demanded more sacrificial giving than I had ever experienced in any other relationship. I continually gave up my body, my sleep, control over my time. The relationship was all about meeting the baby's needs. And yet, out of these acts of sacrificial love, my love for this baby grew deeper and deeper. It's the closest I've ever come to understanding God's sacrificial love. And all his promises about love: that we receive out of our giving.

This ongoing cycle of giving and receiving reminds me of a ditty I saw years ago that continues to dance through my head.

> The love in your heart wasn't put there to stay,
> Love isn't love 'til you give it away.

We want to keep this family-circle cycle going—even through the bumpiest, messiest of times—because guess what? No matter how old we are or how deep the supply of love in our hearts, we all continue to experience those parching longings and loneliness that remind us of our ongoing need to love and be loved.

At times, we may seek to meet that need with things other than loving relationships. For kids, it might be video

---

"We love because he first loved us."
~ 1 John 14:19

---

games. For me, it can be shopping (better known as "retail therapy") or chocolate. Other substitutes might include excessive eating or drinking, or watching endless television, especially soaps that pull us into other people's dramatic searches for love. Or worse, drugs or pornography. Like sugary drinks that are sweet on the tongue for only a moment, these substitutes don't quench our deeper thirsts; they only cause us to thirst again and then search again for something that satisfies our need for security and significance.

So, back to the family and the ways love is passed around the circle through relationships. Let's start with the marriage relationship.

Mommy-Daddy Love

If you're married, you know that your love for each other overflows and permeates your whole family—"for better or for worse." You've probably heard the saying that "the best thing you can do for your kids is to love your spouse." There's a trickle-down theory here about the contagious qualities of love. The whole family responds to the way mom and dad act with each other. Do your children know you love each other? Are you real in your relationship? Can you disagree—lovingly and safely? Do you have fun together? Do you go away alone together, for dinner or a whole weekend?

We know that children change a marriage and can throw the relationship out of whack for a while. Some moms have been honest enough to admit that they are overwhelmed by the amount of love they feel for a new baby. "If I am honest," one mother said, "I think that I love my child more than I love my husband."

I experienced this kind of emotion, and Lynn admits he sometimes felt left out of the obvious intimate bond between me and our children. But one of the surprises of having a child was seeing my husband as a father. Discovering this new and tender part of him deepened my love for him. Probably I didn't tell him that enough, and there were still periods of time when we just endured our way through the feelings of distracted and disconnected love.

My friend Lisa describes the reality of her marriage with young children as "busy love" when all the "life stuff gets in the way and crowds out the places where spontaneous romance once thrived. But our marriage is still there. . . . It still has a pulse." The key is to keep our finger on the pulse.

For some, the challenge is to find balance in the family relationships and be sure that love for a child does not cover up a deeper longing or problem that we refuse to face.

I now know that I love Lynn differently than I love our children, and our married love needs to be nurtured, just as our parent-child love needs to be nurtured. As our children married and started having children of their own, I thought about the ways Lynn and I tried to nurture and balance our married love within the context of our family circle.

Invest in each other: Your mate is not the same person today as the day you walked down the aisle at your wedding. You are each growing and changing as your family grows and changes. Your relationship demands the investment of your time if you want to grow and change together. Lynn and I needed time away alone together to break through the surface stuff and family maintenance issues to get into the deeper soul issues that kept us intimately connected.

Accept your mate; don't expect to change him. It's been said that "opposites attract—until they get married." That's reflected in the show title "I Love You, You're Perfect! Now Change." Remember the qualities that attracted you to your husband when you first met? Do you still appreciate those qualities, or do you try to change them? I did (and sometimes still do!). When we first met, I loved Lynn's mature and disciplined approach to life because he balanced my totally opposite responses. Within the first year of marriage, I was trying to get him to break out of the very molds that attracted me to him. When we live with our differences, we often start "mothering" our husbands by trying to correct and change them (easy to do when that's the way we treat our kids!). Accept him!

Celebrate each anniversary! Our anniversary was the annual date on the calendar when we were committed to getting away alone together. Even if it was just an overnight at a local hotel, we took advantage of the celebration. Such an escape is not only good for you as a couple, it passes an important message on to your children.

Surround yourselves with pictures of the two of you taken on vacations, anniversaries, in the backyard. Frame them and put them on your desk, on a shelf in the family room, on the refrigerator door, or in your bedroom. Good pictures serve as visual aids of your love.

Tell your love story: Make sure your children know how and when you met. Bring out your wedding album. Keep remembering why you married each other, and tell your children why.

Practice kindness: By dinnertime on many days, we've simply run out of kindness. Marriage is about knowing and being known. The secret to loving another person well is to know what pleases that person and then to choose it. Pick up a copy of his favorite magazine. Go along on the errand to the hardware store because that matters to him. Leave him enough hot water for a good shower. You know lots of ways to offer acts of kindness that matter to him.

Grow closer to God together: I've seen an illustration of marriage as a triangle with God at the top point and the husband and wife on the opposite corners at the base of the triangle. As husband and wife inch their way up the sides toward God, the caption explains, "The closer we grow to God; the closer we grow to each other."

Daddy-Style Love

Whether you are married to the father of your children or not, you know that Daddy-style love is different from Mommy-style love. Dads throw kids up in the air; moms snuggle them close. Dads give them pizza and cookies for breakfast. And when he accidentally pulls the tape off the diaper—no problem! He duct tapes the diaper together. Dads care about their children's success; moms care about their happiness. Dads and moms express love differently. That's what God intends in families because kids need different kinds of love.

So we need to zip our lips and let dads be different without always telling them their way is the wrong way. Especially when it doesn't really matter. I was thinking of this the other night when Lynn cut a cantaloupe in half . . . the wrong way. Everyone knows you cut a cantaloupe through the fat middle, like a lemon or lime, instead of end to end the long way, like a watermelon. Everyone except Lynn.

"That's the wrong way," I told him.

Whereupon he responded, "Why does it matter?"

I had to think. Really, his way didn't change the taste of the cantaloupe, which is what mattered. The episode reminded me of all those times I told him "that's the wrong way" as a daddy because it wasn't the way I would dress the child or play with the child or carry the child. It wasn't my way—but

---

Family means . . .

Knowing you're on the same team.

---

it was his way. This is what I learned: when we hold back from criticizing the differences that don't really matter, we encourage dads to be more involved in being dads. And that's what matters most in Daddy-style love.

Mommy-Style Love

Mommy styles are incredibly and beautifully varied. At my office, I work with a mom of a two-year-old, a single mom of teenagers, and a mom with a twenty-year-old daughter living at home and raising her six-month-old son, to name just a few of my co-workers. Our life circumstances are so different; therefore our styles are different out of necessity. But our passions about mothering and families are exactly the same. We are all crazy about our kids; we want to create the best families possible; and we are dedicated to passing on messages that say, "I love you. You matter. I care."

In fact, many moms tell me that they create their own unique ways to say "I love you" in their families. A secret kiss for each child. "We kiss our thumbs and then put them together." Or "we sing the Barney Song together. 'I love you, you love me. . . .'" Or they have special hand squeezes, three for "I love you," four squeezes back for "I love you too." Or giant family sandwich hugs with everyone squeezed together.

As mothers, we recognize how maternal love can fill us with both the highest of heart-bursting highs and the lowest of frustrating lows. All within the same hour. With plenty of guilt wedged in between. But we're also aware of the balance we need in our lives, and we're probably more aware of our personal needs than our own mothers were. What we know for certain is that family matters. And love matters most in our families, and we greatly influence the shape of that love. The giving and receiving.

Family-Style Love

Family-style love comes from the overflow of love poured into each individual's heart. It surrounds and connects the group, and in healthy families, it builds those feelings of significance and security that meet our greatest needs.

"My family was like a circle of mirrors that reflected my self-worth back to me," a mom said. "The way they expressed their love became the way I saw myself. Their love shaped me."

Family-style love grows with giving and receiving, and there's always enough of it to welcome a second (or third or fourth) child or stepchild, stepsibling, stepparent or in-law. I love my friend Lori's description of bringing their newly adopted baby home from China. Her three older children, including a seventeen-year-old ("I'm almost outta here") son, have embraced this baby with a contagious tenderness that has permeated their whole family. "It's better than I ever imagined!" Lori exclaims.

Here's another mom's description of family-style love. "My husband and I have a blended family of five children, ages three to fifteen. What matters most in our household is sitting down to a family-style 'pass-the-mashed-potatoes' kind of meal where the kids take turns blessing the meal and our family."

Family-style love holds the family together—no matter what. It is firm enough to uphold the values that matter and strong enough to give the family hope during disappointing or painful circumstances.

A mom shared this card she got from her autistic son: "When I was not very old, my mommy hugged me a lot. I did not like it, and sometimes I would cry. But she would still hug me. . . . I am different than most kids, but my mommy does not care. She talks to me all day, and prays for me at night. . . . There is one more thing. I can't read or write, so my daddy is looking into my eyes and writing down what I want to say. . . . I LOVE YOU, MOMMY."

Family-style love is fluid enough to make room for each person's growth toward their own dreams. It doesn't assume that "if you love me you will be just like me" or that "you must earn my love." It is the just-right kind of love that does not underlove or overlove. Underloving means holding back on love so that everyone goes their own way and does their own thing, disconnecting the individuals. Overloving drowns the family in love that stifles the growth of individuals within the family.

I remember the bittersweet day when Kendall, our youngest daughter, started kindergarten. For days she had packed and unpacked the contents of her backpack. Some crayons ("I'll make you a picture," she promised); a quarter in a tiny purse ("In case I need to call you"); and a picture of her brother and sister ("If someone doesn't know who they are"). My precious girl-baby was ready to head off into a world that didn't include me. I wondered whether I was ready as I walked with her down our long driveway, along with her older brother and sister. She chattered on excitedly until the big yellow school bus lumbered to a stop by our mailbox. Then she took her sister's hand and turned only momentarily. "'Bye, Mom!" she said confidently. I stooped down to hug her tight . . . and then let her go.

As I look back on that moment, I realize that kind of hug is symbolic of the way we express our love to our children. Though we may be tempted to hug and hold on, we know that the hug that lets go helps to launch the child with confidence.

Family-style love overflows from the reservoir of love in our hearts. It permeates family members, in different levels at different times, offering strength and hope and permanence. Through thick and thin. 'Til death do us part.

After thirty-some years on the job, this is what I've learned about family-style love.

Big love adds up in little ways: When I asked our children how they knew they were loved, their answers weren't about the big vacations or big gifts. Their answers were about the little, everyday things: Taking care of me when I was sick. Reading *Runaway Bunny* at bedtime (where the mother bunny tells her little one that no matter where he goes, she'll be there). Picking me up at school (especially if you were on time). Taking me to the store for cookie dough. Letting me be in 4-H. Putting love notes in our lunches.

Other twentysomethings had similar answers about their family memories. Singing lullabies. Dad showing up at school to eat hot lunch with me. Family hugs. Bread with butter and sugar on top. Little everyday gestures add up to memories of feeling loved in big ways.

Love isn't always easy and doesn't always feel good: Family-style love is not always easy, especially at three o'clock in the morning when the only one sleeping like a baby is daddy, who doesn't know you are pacing the floor with a colicky baby. (Remember what I said in the introduction about our efforts feeling invisible?) And love can bring out the worst instead of the best in us. We find that the person who fills us up with love can also deplete us. We learn that the baby whom we thought would respond to our touch refuses to be soothed. We discover that a spouse or parent or sibling or cousin is sometimes hard to love.

On a much deeper level, love can hurt. "Whenever you choose to love, you're also choosing your greatest pain," said a parent whose five-week-old adopted son was reclaimed by his birth mother. "We choose love, knowing that pain may follow, rather than the greater pain of never loving." Love always includes some loss. The loss of a dream or expectation; the pain of letting go.

Family-style love is not a fifty-fifty, equal-give-and-take kind of love. We're always making sacrifices for the good of the group. But again, we have a choice: to see those uneven gestures as part of our "love offering"—or to run away from home. Or from making a choice. (Take it from me: running away never works. We always end up wanting what we're running away from more than what we're running to.)

Family-style love is an everyday choice about learning to love each other, which we will keep learning every single day for the rest of our lives. It's about trying to *act* loving even when we don't *feel* loving. Just like we tell a four-year-old when we're teaching him to be loving to his little sister: "You just gotta fake it 'til you make it!"

Love takes time: We hear the endless debate about whether quality or quantity time matters most. What matters most is family time together, which demands both. It's kind of like eating. We know that eating matters. In fact, it's key to our health. Sometimes we zoom through fast food; sometimes we prepare and sit and savor a meal for hours. Both happen, with different amounts of quality and quantity, and both add up to eating, which matters!

Same with time together as a family. We know hanging out together is important. On some days we grab quick snatches

---

Family is . . .
**A group of people who know your faults
and choose to love you anyway.**

---

of all-together time. Other days, we spend hours on end together. Different amounts of quality and quantity, but they both add up to spending time together, which is key to our health as a family! Either way, here are a couple of time-sensitive suggestions: seize the season you're in, and seize the moment you're in, so you can be totally present wherever you are. Also, seize the daily moments with the most potential, like mealtimes and bedtimes.

I learned about making the most of the season you're in at a roadside fruit stand from a woman I now call the great Peach Philosopher. Lynn and I were driving through western Colorado after delivering one of our children to a camp, and I was in a nostalgic mood. Our kids were growing up and going off to camps and becoming increasingly independent.

"The peaches are great," the jovial Peach Philosopher encouraged when we pulled off the road in front of her fruit stand. "Try one," she continued, handing us each a thick, juicy slice.

"Yummmm," we agreed, trying to decide how many to purchase.

"Get a whole bushel," she urged, "and eat your fill. That way, you won't have any regrets when peach season is over."

As we drove away with a bushel on the backseat, I knew she'd given me a tip for life. Seize and savor the moments of the season you're in. That way, you'll have fewer regrets when this season ends.

Family rules shape love: When our children were toddlers, Lynn began telling them we had three family rules in our house: (1) tell the truth, (2) think of others, and (3) remember where you came from. The first two explain themselves, but the third one took a bit of coaching. It means to remember who you are and remember what matters most in the family you belong to. Stick together and help each other. To this day, our three children can still repeat our three family rules.

Rules give children security. You've probably heard of the experiment with children on a playground. Without a fence creating a safe boundary, the children huddled together and played only in the middle of the playground. When the fence was constructed, the children played on the whole playground, because the clear boundary made them feel safer and gave them greater freedom. A few family rules give children a sense of security.

"I'm thankful now that you had the confidence to be firm with us, remaining consistent even when it made you unpopular," my daughter Lindsay recently said. "You didn't let us quit things like piano or swim team just because we didn't feel like doing it anymore. I didn't appreciate that then, but now I recognize that you loved us enough to know that pleasing us all the time was not the most important thing."

Love gives back: I know a mom who—with her husband—came up with a unique way to affirm their children and celebrate their ability to overcome obstacles or endure suffering. The parents created an official Hofmann Family Victory Award Book, now filled with several certificates of achievement. The first award went to their five-year-old son, Jason, several years ago for

Character he developed these past six weeks
as he wore a cast on his broken arm.
He persevered with patience and grace.
He learned from a painful fall how to go through real life.
He is an example to each of us how to go through
something difficult so well.

Since the Victory Award Book was created, both their boys have come up with Victory Awards for each of their parents—for courage and perseverance in a big bike race; for courage and stamina in a new job. The award is made at a special family dessert, and according to the mom, "The best part of this tradition is that we are always looking for Victory Award qualities in each other." This family is giving love back to each other in a way that keeps the endless cycle of love flowing around the family circle.

Our imperfect love is good: One of the most important things I've learned about giving and receiving love in our families is that we won't do it all right—and that's good. Though we love each other more than words can describe (at least most of the time), we still love imperfectly. We leak love out of each other's reservoirs and feel guilty about that. But guess what? Our children learn an important life lesson from our imperfect love. As they learn to live with our admitted imperfections—still knowing that we are committed to loving each other as well as we can—they are better able to face the reality of imperfect relationships in the world around them. Our imperfect love also helps them recognize the longing in their hearts for the only one who will love them perfectly . . . Jesus.

Love around the Family Table

I don't want to sound like a know-it-all, but I do know this. In our family, the best place to regularly dish out family-style love has been around the family table. Think about it. Even

---

1 Corinthians 13 Gives Us God's Definition of Love

I always felt overwhelmed with this description because it points out my inadequacies. But I recently heard that this isn't a "how-to" verse. It's a "point to" verse. It points us to the source of this kind of love.

Love is very patient and kind, never jealous or envious, never boastful or proud, never haughty or selfish or rude. Love does not demand its own way. It is not irritable or touchy. It does not hold grudges and will hardly even notice when others do it wrong. It is never glad about injustice, but rejoices whenever truth wins out. If you love someone you will be loyal to him no matter what the cost. You will always believe in him, always expect the best of him, and always stand your ground in defending him.

All the special gifts and powers from God will someday come to an end, but love goes on forever.

1 Corinthians 13:4–8 TLB

---

as a visual aid, the family table represents a place where each person in the family has a place. A totally official (though usually never officially assigned) seat saved just for that person, even if that person isn't there.

If we believe what the experts tell us, the sense of connectedness that happens around the family table meets our deep longing for belonging. This feeling of belonging grows an internal desire to do what is right when it comes to moral behavior, which is more powerful than a fear of consequences if one does wrong. Desire, which grows out of the connection to a caring family, is more powerful and consistent than the fear of authority.

Do you remember the family table of your childhood and where each person sat? Ours was a fancy, oblong, glass table, which represented its own story in our family. It was part of a whole houseful of exquisite French Provincial furniture my mother inherited from an old-maid aunt who lived in Denver. The inheritance surprised our family, and my parents had decided to sell it all, because the fancy furniture certainly didn't fit our lifestyle nor the rambling ranch home that we four children had decorated with the lived-in look. "If we brought that furniture into our home, we'd have to hang a braided silk cord across the door," my father said.

My mother agreed, adding that the sale would help send us all to college. But before they signed the final papers, my parents took us to see the house of treasures. We had visited this eccentric, elderly relative a few times before, but this time was different. We burst through her front door with our usual enthusiasm but then slowed to an awed walk as we crossed through the living room into the formal dining room, suddenly stilled and mesmerized by the beauty of the rugs and the unique glass table.

"Wow . . ."

My parents changed their minds after that visit, deciding what that furniture would bring to our family was far more valuable and longer lasting than the unexpected windfall of money. So that's how we acquired our family table, which my mother insisted set a genteel tone for family meals with four rambunctious children. I don't remember as much about the food served on that table as the details of where each person sat and the fact that we gathered there as a family, even if everyone couldn't make it.

Then there was the table we had when our children were growing up. A heavy, wooden trestle table with a bench along the back wall so we could add extra people without adding extra chairs. Dinnertime was our family time. It wasn't always easy. It wasn't even always pleasant with spilled milk and picky eaters and far too many conversations about bodily functions (complete with sound effects). But dinner marked a special spot in the day, kind of like the comma between afternoon and evening. It was the one time of day when the plural became singular. We said grace together. We passed the salt. We shared feelings and failures and funny stuff.

Eating together regularly is a habit formed early in children's lives, with great benefits. Children who eat with their

Family means . . .
Knowing someone is always in your corner.

parents are said to have better social and verbal skills and are more emotionally stable. They do better in school and are less likely to be involved in drug use or sexual activity. The reason goes back to that sense of belonging and connection that creates the desire to do what is right. The time together communicates that parents care and want to know what their kids are doing in life.

In spite of those compelling facts, we easily get pulled apart with late-afternoon activities and carpools, especially as kids grow up. We end up eating on the run, letting kids microwave their own meals whenever they're hungry. Before we know it, FFY becomes a common dinner plan: Fend For Yourself.

"I grew up in a home with a divorced mother who didn't cook," a mom wrote. "I ate lots of mac 'n' cheese alone. I dreamed how I was going to do better for my child. I wanted her to see mommy and daddy together at the table as we passed the peas. My husband works late and gets home right before our daughter goes to bed, so we have a bedtime snack together. It's not exactly what I envisioned, but we're still providing a time for our daughter to develop her identity within the frame of our family."

Family-style love happens naturally around the family table, which becomes a symbol of our connection. The family table can even carry a legacy into the next generation. The oblong, glass table from our childhood now lives at my sister's house in California. Our wooden trestle table is stored in the rafters of our garage, because Derek wants it for his family as soon as they have a space large enough for it.

Though our children are grown, gathering around the table is still one of our favorite things to do. On weekend nights, we sometimes get a call from one of our children who live within a thirty-minute drive. "Busy for dinner tonight?" We love to pull together a spontaneous meal and sit around the table. As I look back, I think our family table times were key to our continuing closeness today.

What matters most in your family?

That's a no-brainer for most of us. It's the love—learned and lived out in our growing and changing relationships. Because love meets our greatest needs . . . and grows our family from good to great.

Wonderings

1. Draw a picture of the place of longing in your own heart. What experience(s) of love have been poured in there this week? What has leaked the love out?

2. "I love you. You matter. I care." These are important messages of love. Name three specific ways you are giving those messages to your family today.

3. Daddy-style love is different from Mommy-style love. What are some ways you notice this, and how can you help your child's daddy be successful as a dad?

4. Underloving means being so busy and distracted that everyone goes their own way and does their own thing. Overloving means being overprotective or overcontrolling, which smothers people's growth. Is either an issue in your family? Explain.

5. "The love in your heart wasn't put there to stay / Love isn't love 'til you give it away." What does this mean to you when it comes to your family?

"Love each other as I have loved you."
~ John 15:12

5

Fun

Fun Makes Us Want to Be Together

During the most recent summer Olympics, my friend Lou and her family created their own backyard version of the Olympic games, complete with judges, patriotic music, and festive awards ceremony. Then they invited friends over to team up for the events: badminton, bocce, croquet, and horseshoes. The adults competed. The kids judged. Awards were given for Most Passionate, Funniest, and Best Teamwork in a mock ceremony staged on a big rock. The recipients received Olympic medals, flowers, and goofy pictures of themselves.

For years, this same family hosted a live nativity in their front yard at Christmastime, giving out flyers and inviting all their neighbors to attend. The stable included a miniature horse and lambs and even a pot-bellied pig. Neighborhood kids acted out the Christmas story, and everyone sang Christmas carols. This family also hosted pumpkin-carving parties, scavenger hunts, and neighborhood potlucks.

If you telephone this family today, you will be greeted with some humorous or dramatic message, recorded by one of the daughters. They regularly plan margins of do-nothing time into their days so they have space for spontaneous family fun, like playing cards, going on a hike, or cooking dinner together. Does this family know how to have fun or what? According to Lou, "Fun makes our family want to be together." According to her daughter, "Fun makes me more fun to be around." According to their neighbors, this family's fun brings the neighborhood together.

Fun matters to this family.

Family Fun Matters

Fun is like the frosting on the family cake. It makes family life lots more yummy and enticing. It creates the unique personality that characterizes a family, just like the sparkly decorations sprinkled on luscious frosting. It's the rich sweetness that keeps children and parents coming back for more.

I love fun. I see it as the most beckoning part of the five-star qualities. And probably the easiest for me to embrace. A part of my heart has never grown up, and having children feeds that part. I not only love to lavish the frosting onto our family cake, I love to pass around the bowl and join in as we all lick it clean. Smeary, messy, chocolate faces and all. I love to plan surprises. Surprise parties (a big thirty-ninth birthday party for Lynn . . . a surprise because everyone expects that on their fortieth birthday). Surprise meals (anyone for green mashed potatoes?). Surprise visits (flying a favorite ten-year-old cousin into town and having her knock on our front door).

Surprises are contagious in a family. Years ago when I wrote my first book, a friend hosted a book-signing party. My brother Dexter, who also lives in Boulder, showed up with a homeless person (not a surprise for this brother who easily befriends strangers). After getting his friend something to eat, the two of them approached the table where I sat signing books.

"I want to introduce you to my friend Frank," Dexter said.

"Any friend of Dexter's is a friend of mine," I said as Frank, who was wearing dirty gloves, reached for a book on the table. Something in the hand gesture looked familiar in a way that caught my breath, and I gasped as I looked up at Frank, hat pulled down low over his face. It was my sister, Joan, from

---

Family means...

Knowing where the *good* ice cream is kept.

California, who successfully pulled off this memorable surprise. Of course, that's when the real celebration started at that party.

We know the importance of fun and play in a child's life. Play is the way children discover and understand their world and relationships. It stimulates the imagination. With fascination, I used to watch our children play "let's pretend" games. The dark hole between the couch and chair in a blanket fort became a secret hideaway, and a little sister became a monster or a mommy, depending on the game. Childhood play is said to be foundational to adult happiness. Play and fun is equally foundational to family healthiness.

Fun sweetens our lives: Family fun is not just something we do in life. It's an attitude we have about life. Translated, this attitude means that we see life as basically good; our cups are half-full (not half-empty); and we have plenty to celebrate, even on dreary days.

Fun recognizes that kids are both funny and fun and that they infuse a family with a contagious playfulness that invites others to join in. Fun also sweetens up the not-so-sweet stuff in life. Lynn's parents, who were in their nineties, died within eleven days of each other (a testimony to the depth of their love!). Our cousins brought their children to the first funeral. These kids, all under five years old, were perfectly quiet during the service and had a grand time at the reception in the church's large all-purpose room. Eleven days later, when they learned of the second death, they exclaimed, "Wow! We get to go to another funeral!" Lynn's parents would have loved that reaction.

Fun turns monotonous tasks like folding laundry into a game of "finding my clothes in the pile." The search for a lost shoe becomes a treasure hunt. The dread of getting ready for bed becomes a race to beat the ding on the timer-clock. Or a game that puts all the stuffed animals to bed so the toddler has to go night-night too.

Fun creates its own unique style of communication within a family. My friend Joyce tells about her family's made-up code language. For instance, when company came to dinner, her mom would pass the pot roast around, offering seconds, but in passing the platter to her own children she would say, "Would you like some—PMK?" (Plenty more in the kitchen . . . which meant "help yourselves.") Or she'd say, "Would you like some more—FHB?" (Family hold back!) That code language is now being passed on to the third generation.

Fun turns ho-hum into WOW! Breakfast is ho-hum, but making pancakes in the shape of the letters in their names is WOW. Doing a bunch of errands together is ordinary, but putting in a CD of kids' praise songs and singing together as loud as we can makes the car ride extra-ordinary. Dinner is ho-hum, but a spontaneous picnic with takeout tacos is WOW!

Fun becomes our common ground: Fun lets us enter each other's worlds. Our kids did love building those blanket forts in their "let's pretend" world, but when I climb into their blanket fort, I enter their world, and our shared experience bonds us. Same is true when I sit cross-legged on the floor, eye-to-eye with a two-year-old, singing "Itsy Bitsy Spider" with all the hand motions. Fun ties generations together. A thirty-eight-year-old father told me about the experience of skiing with his sixty-eight-year-old father and eight-year-old son. "What fun we had!" he beamed. Fun opens a larger world to our children . . . a world of sports, drama, music, science, history, and travel.

Fun is the playful way we express our love for each other: We used to play "how much do I love you?" games. (The answer is "wider than . . . higher than . . . deeper than . . ." all the random things you can think of.) Nicknames are fun, when they are meant to be loving and are lovingly received by the recipient. Same is true of teasing. The rule in our family was that we couldn't tease about physical appearance, because that's the place we're all most vulnerable (including me). For good reason . . . all humor is based on truth. The general rule is, if the other person doesn't think it's funny, then it's not. Family nicknames and appropriate teasing are fun ways to deepen our sense of belonging in a family, because appropriate teasing says, "I know you so well that I know how to tease you in the right way. I know what you think is funny too."

Fun makes memories that keep us wanting more: Fun is addictive. My friend Lou, whose family created the summer Olympics party, said that she wants her girls to want to spend time with the family rather than away from the family. As I listen to our kids start into their "remember when's," they mostly remember the fun times (even if they included some disasters). "Remember when we went on that vacation and couldn't turn the car off because the diesel engine wouldn't start again?" "Remember when we took the puppy on the hike and had to carry him all the way down the mountain?" (I certainly remember that one, because I said we shouldn't take the puppy and got overruled, so I tried so hard not to say "I told you so" all the way down the mountain.) "Remember when we went on that backpacking trip with the Hutchens, and we all laid down by the lake on blankets and watched shooting stars?" Fun makes memories that feed our hungry souls and keep enticing us back for more.

Fun creates a legacy that is passed on from generation to generation: My mother had a great sense of humor, but I thought she was sometimes just plain goofy. When emphysema began taking its toll on her, she learned to compensate for her lack of mobility. For instance, she had a horn installed in our car that sounded like a moose, so if she had to let a child know she was waiting, that child recognized her honk! When I was living in a college dormitory, she sometimes stopped by—and blew her horn. "Carol, your mother is here!" my friends told me upon hearing the moose call.

My kids would swear that some of that goofiness got passed on in the DNA. I've collected a bunch of silly hats, just perfect for the Fourth of July or Thanksgiving or an airport welcome-home celebration. When our daughter Kendall and her fiancé arrived for their wedding, I rounded up a few friends and greeted them at the airport with flowers and a bridal veil, as we sang, "Here Comes the Bride"! Kendall feigned total embarrassment, but she recently greeted a friend at the airport wearing the bridesmaid's dress from that friend's wedding. The goofy-but-fun legacy lives on.

So how is your family fun quotient? How about taking a quick assessment? The key here is fun that involves interaction between family members. Not just passive participation. Your family may be off the charts—or you may get some ideas of ways you can add more fun to your lives! Give yourself a point for each activity that applies.

____ You make up your own unique family celebrations, like Pajama Day or Backward Day or a birthday party for the family pets.

____ You have a unique family message on your answering machine.

____ Birthdays are big at your house.

____ Watching movies together is more than watching movies. It involves things like sleeping bags, snacks, and snuggles.

____ You sometimes eat breakfast together, like on Saturday mornings.

____ You play games together.

____ Family traditions matter.

____ When your kids make up games, you play by their rules.

____ You have a favorite family television show that you watch and talk about together.

____ You all get in the car and go somewhere together at least once a week.

____ Family vacations matter.

____ You have a dress-up box of goofy, fun clothes and hats.

____ You regularly read books out loud together.

____ You have a family-favorite sports team that makes you jump up and down.

Within the last year, you have . . . (one point each)

____ Visited a park with swings and a slide.

____ Surprised your family with some goofy spontaneous activity, like late one evening, piling everyone in the car and going off to your favorite ice cream store in your pajamas.

____ Flown kites together.

____ Laid on the grass and looked at the stars.

____ Gone bowling.

____ Hosted a family talent show.

____ Played miniature golf.

____ Gone on a family treasure hunt.

____ Served a surprising meal, like a lunch of banana splits.

____ Created a funny family video.

____ Put a big picture puzzle together.

____ (Add your own.)

Out of a possible high of twenty-six, how did you score? Anything above fifteen and you're doing pretty well in the family fun department. If you'd like to score higher, it's never too late to reach for that five-star quality and lighten up. That's the surest way to raise your family fun quotient.

Lighten Up

Lightening up means not taking yourself too seriously. It means knowing what matters most and choosing what matters most. And it increases our potential for family fun.

Lighten up on yourself: I love to play, but I face one ongoing challenge: a persistent voice in my head that tells me I shouldn't play until I get all my work done. Or when I do stop to play, I feel guilty. (But most of us are so ready for guilt that we even feel guilty for not feeling guilty when we don't feel guilty!) I'm old enough now to know that I will never get all my work done. In fact, I will surely die with an unfinished "to do" list. So I need to learn to play in the midst of unfinished work.

Remember recess in school? Recess is based on the same idea of stopping to play in the midst of working because that's good for us. So why don't we keep up that good-for-us rhythm? To do so, we need to recognize the value of family fun and place it higher on our list of priorities. It may mean making a "to do" list and a "to don't" list, with all the things we don't have to do, in order to have time to play. We have to practice playing in order for playing to become a more natural habit. Then we have to focus (and sometimes force) ourselves to be in the "play moment" by being where we are when we're there. To take advantage of playtime.

Lighten up on your standards: "I want my kids to re-member that we played together and made time for them, not that mom was a crazy house cleaner!" one mom said. Many of us relate. I don't know when cleanliness got next to godliness, but many of us have an unrealistic expectation when it comes to how clean our homes should look. Like they're not even lived in! These expectations keep us from having fun because we're worried about the messes that fun makes. Like the kitchen that will be splattered with flour if we make cookies with the kiddies. Even the mess of all those blankets and makeshift anchors to hold them down in making the blanket forts. I have to admit, I've always had a hard time being cheerful in the middle of a mess that I'm going to have to clean up. No finger painting with chocolate pudding in our house!

When I was in college, I learned a phrase I still try to apply to my own unrealistic standards. It's "C+ works." A roommate and I were pulling an all-nighter, studying for a test, when she suddenly flipped her book closed at about midnight. "I just decided . . . C+ works," she said with great conviction. With that, she went off to bed.

This healthy attitude about learning to live with "average" takes practice for some of us who grew up pursuing As, not only on our report cards, but in other areas of our lives as well. For instance, when I went back to work after being at home with our kids for many years, I tried to do everything I'd always done each morning—in lots less time. Prayer time. Breakfast. Unload the dishwasher. Load it back up. Clean up the clutter. Make the bed. Except I couldn't get everything done. My husband, Lynn, was plenty willing to help. I just had to be plenty willing to accept the way the dishwasher was loaded or the way the pillows were placed

---

Family means . . .

You don't always have to put your best foot forward.

---

on the bed. Did those things *really* matter? No. C+ works! C+ often works when looking for the perfect wrapping paper or birthday card or making cookies with the kiddies. They don't have to be the perfect "from scratch" kind. They can be the slice and bakes (no flour that way). And the kitchen can be "C+ clean" lots more often. Practicing that attitude leaves more opportunity for fun.

Lighten up on the idea that you have to play a certain way: Playing comes more easily for some people than others, and there's certainly more than one way to have fun with your family. Your family's way may not be the same as your friends'. Their family might always be on the go, swimming, riding bikes, or kicking soccer balls in the backyard. Your style may be quieter, reading books together, playing board games, or going on slow-paced walks together. One mom said that she and her husband both work, so their family time is quiet time. Hunkering down and hanging out in the family room on a Friday night to eat pizzas and watch a movie is their idea of family fun. Another family considers their "chill time" every night as fun time. "All three of us cozy up in our big chair and read bedtime stories." The activity isn't nearly as important as the time spent together doing something fun.

Maybe you have to work at playing. Maybe board games make you bored! Or you get tired of reading the same book or putting the same puzzle together for the tenth time. Or you don't like playing "action figures" when your son is telling you to make the *Kabonk!* noises just like him. "Sometimes we do things as a family because one of us really enjoys it," one mom says. "My daughter likes to play dress-up and dress the rest of us up. My son likes to hold my hands and jump in the pool . . . over and over again. I get tired of it, but I do it because he enjoys it."

Other parents may take charge and make up new rules or rewrite the story, changing the action figures into robbers who take candy from the candy store and end up gobbling up all the candy to destroy the evidence and then get very sick and then feel very sorry they took the candy. (Of course there must be a moral to the story.)

You don't have to be totally right-brain creative to have fun as a family. You don't have to make up new ideas. Borrow some from other families who have fun together. Watch a preschool teacher or Sunday school teacher play with children. Watch your children at play and simply join in.

Ways to Play

Maybe you need a few good ideas to jump-start your family fun. It starts with you, mom. Having your own playtime increases your playfulness, which ultimately helps you shape your family's fun. I recently gathered a bunch of family-fun ideas from moms, which I've added to my own time-tested suggestions.

Mom play: When our kids were growing up, tennis was my mom-time, fun-time activity. I took lots of grief for it, because our kids enjoyed playing the martyr role in this picture. They loved complaining about spending time around the pool with a babysitter at our neighborhood tennis club. I absorbed their comments with the assurance that the activity was good for all of us. I now know it was good for me. As the mom of young children, tennis was the one area of my life where I could measure my progress. If I practiced my serve for thirty minutes, I saw improvement. If I played well, I sometimes won a gold plastic trophy for my efforts.

I got kind of addicted to those gold plastic trophies. The more I got, the more successful I felt, though I soon realized that nobody needs a shelf full of gold plastic trophies. But for that season in my life, playing tennis was my fun and made me more fun, in spite of our children's mock complaints that have only grown more mockingly exaggerated through the years. . . . "Remember when mom used to leave us at the swimming pool with the babysitter from dawn until after dark with only a few soggy peanut butter and jelly sandwiches?" Appropriate teasing because I laugh too. But they also learned how to play tennis during those times. And gathered some trophies of their own. Family fun!

One mom describes her fun as putting on a pink tutu and going off to a midweek ballet class, which plunks her down in a whole different world and lightens her attitude. Other moms gather regularly for an evening or even a whole weekend of scrapbooking. "This is fun," one mom explained, "because my family is staring at me through the pictures I am cutting and putting into the scrapbook. They are far away, but still present . . . so it's a perfect mom's getaway." Other moms find fun singing in a choir or participating in a drama group. The point is to do something that nurtures your own playfulness. In a roundabout way, that increases your family fun quotient.

Mom-kid play: Many moms describe how they try to create fun in the midst of difficult days—or nights. One Friday, Donna found herself in Wal-Mart at two o'clock in the morning with three preschool-aged daughters squished into her cart. The adventure started out as innocent fun. Her husband travels frequently, and to make the separations more bearable, they always plan a fun family reunion at the airport, no matter what time dad returns. On this particular night, his flight from Alaska to Savannah was due in about 12:30 a.m. So she and her three little pajama-clad daughters showed up, only to discover his plane was delayed. Not enough time to go all the way back home. Way too much time to watch the moths on the airport windows and count runway lights. So off they went to the twenty-four-hour Wal-Mart. To get coloring books and crayons, crackers and water, and then back to the airport where three little girls squealed with delight when daddy finally arrived about three in the morning. "My kids and I fell backwards into an adventure and figured out that fun is where—and when—you make it."

Michelle tells about finding fun in the midst of a South Dakota winter "when it gets so cold outside that your breath nearly freezes solid in midair." Her two boys, ages two and four, were bored and "driving each other and me nuts," she describes. "Rescue Heroes again? I can only make-believe so much in one day, and doing the same puzzle for the eleventh time makes me think that forty below zero isn't too cold to go outside after all."

So she got an idea. She told her boys to get their mittens on and wait in the bathroom. "I found a large plastic tub, went outside, and filled it with snow, not one time, but five times! I dumped the snow in the bathtub and let them play just as if they were outside. They were so excited, and the look on their faces told me that the water and mess I would have to clean up would certainly be worth it in the end. Yes, there was water everywhere in the bathroom, and yes, their socks and knees were soaking wet, but later, over hot chocolate, the boys deemed this 'the best day ever.'"

Other moms have brought the outside inside for fun in the winter by putting the kids' plastic wading pool in the living room and filling it with fifty or one hundred pounds of pinto beans. What follows is a child's delight, walking barefoot around in the beans or filling plastic buckets with them and just sifting them through their fingers.

Family fun: One family described their water-balloon fight. Not the ordinary, spontaneous kind, but a well-planned family event, with plenty of ammunition—red, yellow, green, blue, and orange water-filled balloons piled in the backyard. Teams were chosen, and for at least half an hour, this family of four battled around the backyard, cheered on by the neighbors who came out of their houses to watch the battle.

Other families describe spending a whole rainy Saturday in pajamas, watching movies, eating snacks instead of meals, and playing games. More family fun includes regular "quilt nights" or family slumber parties, with mattresses on the floor so everyone can watch movies until they fall asleep. There are mud-puddle walks, birthday parties for make-believe friends or stuffed animals, and mystery trips, including this one planned by the dad in a family of four.

The family had recently relocated to New Jersey, so the dad, concerned that his wife was missing their former home, made this suggestion one Saturday morning. "How about you close your eyes and flip through the pages of this book of *New Jersey Day Trips*, and we'll head to whatever place your finger lands." The mom worried about the two-year-old twins' nap schedule and finding clean restrooms for the newly potty-trained pair when they shrieked, "Pee pee's coming!" But she pushed those thoughts aside, closed her eyes, flipped through the pages, and landed on a page describing a place on the New Jersey shore. Off they went on what turned out to be a fabulous family outing.

"Whenever the weather gets above ninety degrees, we have a barefoot evening," another mom describes. "Everyone hops in the car (no shoes allowed!). We drive to a local park with a water fountain to play in and grab an ice cream cone or snow cone before coming home. The kids, ages three and five, watch the thermometer in the car, hoping it goes

---

Family means . . .
You never feel left out.

---

above ninety!" On rainy summer evenings, this same family is known to order pizza and eat it in the kids' backyard playhouse. Fun!

Still another family describes the dress-up shows the kids host regularly for their parents and grandparents. The kids commentate themselves down the makeshift runway and even serve fancy finger sandwiches to the audience.

One mom describes turning an ordinary dinner into a surprising, fun adventure with her own rendition of stone soup, featuring a pot of broth with a big stone in the center of the table. She read the *Stone Soup* story to the family as she stirred the soup, and the kids left the table to see what they could find in the refrigerator to add to the soup, just as the characters in the story did, all in an effort to share. This dinner marks National Old Rock Day in this family and represents only one of the many made-up or real holidays this family celebrates. "Why?" you might ask. This mom says, "Because our last two years have been filled with deaths, near deaths, ongoing illness, financial pressures. And our celebrations keep joy and laughter in our family, even as life dishes out challenges."

A single mom, widowed when her children were young, reflects on how she opened her world to a different kind of fun than some of her married friends. "My bedroom was like a second family room. We'd all pile into bed and snuggle up to read stories, and it didn't matter if someone fell asleep. We also had lots of spontaneous fun. One year, on a whim, we rented a convertible and drove down the coast on Thanksgiving."

Another single mom said, "After my divorce, Sunday was a difficult day. But then we turned it into the best day! After Sunday school, we played all day long."

Other Fun Ideas

Family fun is regularly experienced through games, birthday celebrations, vacations, traditions, and holiday celebrations, to name just a few ideas. All help us to lighten up and put more play in our days, which matters in a family.

Games: The best family games are those without a coach, practice schedule, or expensive equipment. That's one reason backyard games are making a comeback. Badminton, croquet, horseshoes, and even hopscotch are said to be enjoying a new popularity. There are always huge options with all the indoor games. Games not only promote togetherness, they can also help a child learn to follow the rules, learn patience in playing, and face the risk of losing, all within the safety of the family circle.

Birthdays: Birthdays are a once-a-year gift of a day to celebrate the uniqueness of the person God has created—no matter how old the birthday person is. Everybody expects the traditional cake, candles, and presents at a birthday celebration, but how about some other fun ingredients?

One mom brings out a white birthday tablecloth on her two daughters' birthdays each year, traces that child's hand- and footprints with markers in different shades of pink, and dates the prints. Another mom puts a gift bag of new clothes on the birthday child's bed so he or she has something special to wear. Another writes an annual birthday letter to her child, filled with descriptions of the good ways her child's been growing in the last year. One family I know gives each of their two sons a special, verbal birthday blessing at their birthday celebration each year. "We want them to hear our voices telling them the qualities we see in them and how we see those qualities being part of their lives in the future."

A mother with two grown children still calls each of them on their birthdays, at the exact (daytime!) moment they were born. One mom stretches out the birthday celebration by taking each child out for something special on the date of their birthday each month. (A May fourth birthday means she takes that child out on the fourth of every month.)

Birthday fun isn't limited to kids. When parents celebrate their own birthdays in unique ways, kids see that fun is for the whole family. Letting them help plan birthday parties for dad or mom carries on a family legacy that says, "Hey! We're a birthday family!"

Family vacations: Getting away from home gives families the best chance to play together without the normal distractions. It also gives them an opportunity to learn to get along in new surroundings, like a small motel room with a single bathroom. A vacation offers family fun in three tenses: you look forward to it and plan for it; you enjoy the vacation as you experience it; and then it becomes part of your reservoir of memories. One family makes a habit of choosing a goofy family pose for each vacation, and everywhere they go on that vacation, they strike that pose and take a picture. Another family makes a tradition of mystery vacations. Mom and dad plan the car trip and then give the kids a clue a day, starting a week before vacation. Friends, neighbors, and cousins have started getting into the game, begging to know and promising not to tell, but the destination always remains a mystery until the family starts driving.

Camping vacations are popular. Sitting around a campfire and snuggling together in a tent or camper offer opportunities to bond closely. Too closely for me sometimes. We did our share of camping when our children were young, but I have to admit, I was the first camping dropout in our family. After a few years, I decided that camping always sounds like more fun than it really is. My contact lenses never got

---

Family is . . .

A bunch of people you can't get rid of and eventually realize you don't want to get rid of.

---

clean, fixing meals and cleaning up took way too much time, and for some silly reason, at two o'clock in the morning, all snuggled in our tent, I couldn't get comfortable, so I spent the rest of the night recalling every "bear mauls camper" story I'd ever heard.

I admire the moms who pull it off better than I do, like the mom who says that her family of five plans a new trip every time they go camping. "We explore God's creation together. We bike, swim, play games, and eat lots of food I typically don't allow at home, and it's so nice not to have any phones, PCs, or TVs."

We took vacations with another family when our kids got a bit older. We rented an RV and traveled together like the famous Griswolds to some off-the-beaten-path places for some great adventures. (Including the typical mishaps like taking off part of the roof of the RV when we got it stuck under a low-hanging drive-through. "No problem, just let the air out of the tires," the first helpful person suggested.) On one New Year's Eve, we hiked to the bottom of the Grand Canyon with this family and stayed for two nights.

Traditions: Families pick up and make up their own traditions as they grow. It's part of what uniquely bonds them as a family. I attended a couple's wedding shower recently, and the theme was "traditions." Each guest was asked to bring a gift symbolic of a favorite family tradition, along with an explanation, in order to start this couple off with some ideas for establishing their own traditions. Gifts included a "special-day plate," a breakfast-in-bed tray, a soup tureen along with recipes to make soup on Sunday afternoons, and a bag of candles, balloons, and colorful paper goods with a note to find reasons to celebrate spontaneously and often.

Children often create our family traditions. One family now celebrates Happy Family Day on the third Saturday of each month. "The tradition started when we were rushing around one Saturday morning, getting ready to head to Sam's Club. I was frustrated that the kids were not putting on their shoes and coats; the oldest was giving the youngest an 'atomic wedgie.' In response to my rising stress level, my son said, 'Why get so upset, Mom? You know it's happy family day, and we are supposed to be happy all day long.' Where this came from I have no clue, but for the whole day, we celebrated Happy Family Day . . . and believe it or not, we really were happy all day long."

"Homemade gingersnaps are one of our family traditions," according to my friend Judy. "Our kids like their grandmother's homemade gingersnaps, so I started making them. When their friends came over, I often made gingersnaps, plopping warm gingersnaps into their open hands. One by one, as they went off to college, our kids requested gingersnaps. So did their friends. I always have the ingredients on hand, because we have lots of spontaneous gingersnap moments. At my daughter's recent wedding, she thanked us for gingersnaps in the wedding program."

Christmas is the holiday filled with the most opportunities for family traditions because the season lasts so long. Young families search for just the right traditions to claim as their own. The right birthday celebration for Jesus. The right balance of gifts. The best way to spend the day. Alexandra, my daughter-in-law, said she was looking for the right coffee-cake recipe to become their traditional breakfast on Christmas morning. "Last year's attempt was too much trouble and didn't taste that good," she said.

Families outgrow some traditions or choose to modify some. We used to have an annual family Christmas party, complete with festive food and decorations, an Advent candle-lighting ceremony, a wrapped favor for each child (delivered by Santa Claus), and special music (I usually played my accordion, which is a whole different story, but suffice it to say, most people considered that to be the most

Family is . . .
fun!

humorous part of the party). However, the party's essential ingredients grew more complicated each year. Finally, I realized we'd created our own Christmas monster and knew we either had to settle for less or give up the party altogether. The kids helped downsize the celebration with less food. Fewer gifts. Less mess. The party lasted several more years because we simplified the celebration. (But in case you're wondering, the accordion did survive the cuts; it kept coming back, by popular demand.)

Judy's Gingersnaps

1 cup sugar
¾ cup shortening
¼ cup Brer Rabbit golden molasses
1 egg
2 cups flour
2 teaspoons soda
1 teaspoon ginger
1 teaspoon cinnamon
½ teaspoon salt

Cream sugar and shortening. Add molasses and egg. Stir together dry ingredients and add to creamy mixture. Chill dough for one hour. Roll into small balls and then roll balls in sugar to coat. Bake at 350 degrees for 10–12 minutes. Do not overbake. Remove from oven just after they have "fallen." Enjoy with a cold glass of milk for an old-fashioned treat.

Family fun matters. It's the frosting on our cakes. It comes in lots of different family flavors, always sweetening our lives and enticing us to keep coming back for more and more. Fun takes a family from good to great! And makes us want to be together.

Wonderings

1. What is your favorite childhood memory of family fun?
2. What do you do for "mom fun"?
3. In ten years, what will your kids remember your family did for fun? What are your family's favorite games? What unique family traditions do you have?
4. What keeps you from having fun in your family?
5. "C+ works!" Especially in some areas of our lives (see page 104). In what area of your life might C+ work?
6. Why is fun important to your family?

6

Loyalty

Loyalty Connects Us ... for Always

You see it at soccer games and swim meets.

It's obvious in courtrooms and hospital waiting rooms.

It oozes all around at weddings and funerals and family reunions.

You hear it in "I'm sorry" and "I still love you."

What is "it"?

It's family loyalty. Showing up for each other. Sticking together. Choosing to be there ... no matter what. Persevering, even when life is messy. Because we're family.

We're not born with loyalty. If we were, we would never see sibling rivalry or broken families. We learn loyalty. And then we choose it. Experience by experience.

Loyalty is the little girl sticking up for her big brother at the birthday party. It's the twelve-year-old boy donating bone marrow to his younger sister. Loyalty is the family who hears the "guilty" verdict in that courtroom and says, "We

109

will stand by you." It's choosing to turn toward, rather than away from, each other.

Loyalty is easily learned early in life. It grows out of children's utter dependency upon those closest to them. Naturally, children feel faithful allegiance to the people who love them and keep them safe. Young children become fiercely loyal to their family's favorite sports teams and political candidates and choices of friends. They think what the family thinks.

Children learn loyalty from what they see: support and kindness for each other. Stepping over our own needs to meet the needs of others in the family. We hope they learn to love others well because they have been well loved.

"Loyalty keeps us doing stuff we don't always feel like doing," a mom said. "We drive an hour to visit grandparents on a Sunday afternoon or keep all the cousins and their two dogs for a long weekend so their parents can go away— because we're family."

Loyalty: A Choice

Though loyalty is learned early, in healthy families, loyalty is also recognized as a choice. Otherwise, loyalty can become blind loyalty, the kind that doesn't "see" problems or the value of individuality. "When I was growing up, we pretended our family was perfect and covered up some stuff because that's what it meant to be loyal," a friend told me. "Talking about it would be disloyal."

In healthy families, children are encouraged to become increasingly independent. They learn to make their own choices and may make choices their parents wouldn't make. Parents model appropriate loyalty with the attitude that "we will be there for each other, even if you don't make the same choices

I would make. We may disagree. We may draw boundaries. We may feel and think differently. In fact we *will* be different. But we are committed to remain in relationship. No matter what." Loyalty with a choice becomes commitment.

Loyalty is a choice and commitment that empowers people, especially when facing bumps in a family relationship: "We had some problems in my family growing up," a young mom said, "and I still have some issues with my parents. But I'm choosing to honor them and work through these issues, because I'm committed to our relationship."

Another mom added, "You choose your friends, but family relationships are *given* to you—so you choose to keep investing yourself in those relationships." Loyalty is a choice we make again and again—to be in relationship with each other. It results in a commitment to the family.

Loyalty is a five-star quality learned as a family experiences all the other qualities of love and fun and growth and faith together. It is learned in three places: within the family team; with siblings; and with extended family.

Family Team Spirit

"We want our children to know that it means something special to be a member of this family," one mom said. "We share a unique identity. We even have our own family cheer." Another family describes dressing like a team sometimes. "We may look goofy as we go whooshing down the ski slopes in our matching yellow-and-black jackets, or wearing the same T-shirts at the Fourth of July parade. But for us, for now, it's cool."

These families have team spirit. In sports, a team is a group of individuals bonded together for a single purpose: to win! Team loyalty and spirit come from sharing a passion

Heir Care
by Shelly Radic

I remember summer mornings at the beach, when my fingers nimbly arranged fine strands of little-girl hair into six neat French braids. The half hour spent braiding was well worth the effort, because loose, long, flowing hair becomes painfully tangled when little girls splash in waves and chase seagulls across the sand.

To keep my three girls occupied during the braiding process, I fell into the habit of telling stories of my childhood. My daughters loved hearing about mommy being chased down the street by a mean black dog, creating Barbie villages that stretched across an entire backyard, and the Christmas Eve when a tiny kitten threw up all over my new, blue fur coat. Many mornings they requested to hear my "scar" stories—the time I sliced my kneecap on the edge of a metal slide, ruining my first pair of white knee socks; or when I had to wait in a long line with other little kids and a mean nurse stabbed me in the arm with a giant needle.

Why were my daughters so fascinated by mundane stories of my 1960s childhood? I think it boggled their minds that mommy was once a little girl like them. A little girl afraid of dogs, in love with Barbie, and grossed out by throw-up. A little girl who scraped her knees and cried after shots.

During those early mornings of hair care, my childhood experiences wove together with those of my children, intricately intertwining our lives like the strands of hair in their neat French braids.

for that common purpose and working together to achieve that goal.

Families are like teams with a common purpose. In chapter 2 ("Family Dreams"), you identified some family goals and purposes. This book identifies the five-star qualities of love, fun, loyalty, growth, and faith, which are common goals to pursue together.

Family team spirit grows with shared history and future. Though each generation creates their own history, we also gain a deeper appreciation of who we are from past generations. As Ma said to Pa in John Steinbeck's *The Grapes of Wrath,* "How will our children know who they are if they don't know where they came from?" Visiting the place where a grandparent grew up, passing down the character-quality stories from a different generation or culture because of Italian or German or Vietnamese roots . . . these are ways a family is unified by carrying a common past into the future.

"My mom grew up in a frugal family with nine children. Boy, were they cost cutters!" a mom wrote. "But they are fun-loving people to be around . . . and I think my daughter needs their example just as much as I do because they are a view to a simpler past."

Team spirit and loyalty don't make family problems disappear. The mom whose family sometimes dresses alike admits her team faces bumps. "Like when your sister has a soccer game and a piano recital on your birthday, it's hard to share your day! But all teams must work together. . . . I guess they don't call it teamwork for nothing!"

Challenges help the team pull together. A single mom remembers that right after she and her husband divorced, she and her two young children stuck together like glue in their newly configured family. As they look back on those years now, the children especially remember their mom referring to them as a team. "Okay, team," she'd say. "Let's go."

"When the chips were down," another mother added, "we were always on the same team."

Fan support is important for the family team and includes a larger circle of people who cheer the family toward success. Family fans include our extended families, church family, and close friends who know our heart passions. They celebrate our birthdays and holidays with us; they are there for us in hard times. Their loyal support makes a difference.

Sibling Loyalty

If your family has more than one child, sibling relationships offer life-shaping lessons in Loyalty 101. If you have a single-child family, your child will find similar relational opportunities with cousins or close friends. My daughter-in-law grew up in a single-child family, and she and her cousin are like sisters with a sibling relationship. One mom writes, "I have only one sibling, and he lives in another state, so to give my daughter (an only child) that family-ness, I keep in close touch with my cousins who live closer and have children her age."

Attempts to establish good sibling relationships often begin before a second child is born or adopted into a family—because sibling rivalry is so commonly expected. I've often heard sibling rivalry described this way, just to help moms understand the feelings: Imagine your husband coming home and telling you that he's going to have a second wife. She will be younger and cuter, and she will take lots of his time. But don't worry, because this doesn't mean he will love her more.

Feel the feelings? No wonder sibling rivalry is real and loyalty needs to be learned. No wonder we try to proactively pave the way for the newborn in the family in hopes of establishing a good relationship. "This baby is going to be so happy to have you as a big brother (or sister)," a mom tells her child. When the baby is born, many parents present the sibling with a gift from the new baby, and the sibling is too young to care or question how a helpless baby was able to purchase such a gift.

When a friend discovered she was pregnant with her second child, she began looking around for siblings in other families who seemed to like each other and asked them why they got along. "Because my older brother treated me so well," one teenager said.

As soon as baby number two was born, this mom began telling the older brother, "Your friends will come and go, but you two will always have each other. So you need to treat each other well. Besides," she often added as a mild threat, "your baby brother may grow up to be bigger than you are."

Another mother offered the same kind of positive prophecy to her daughters. "Your little sister will grow up to be the maid of honor at your wedding," she began telling her older daughter shortly after the birth of the younger one.

When our children were young, catching a glimpse of sibling loyalty swelled my heart with love almost as much as tiptoeing into their bedrooms to watch them sleep. An older brother tenderly taking his little sister's hand and walking with her into the doctor's office. An older sister reading to a younger one, until the younger one falls asleep, her head resting on her sister's shoulder.

I often think of the sibling story widely circulated several years ago. A little boy, probably about three or four years old, was so excited about the arrival of his new baby sister, but serious complications developed during delivery, and the baby was placed in the neonatal intensive care unit. "There is very little hope," the parents were told. Instead of celebrating the birth, they found themselves planning a funeral.

The boy kept begging to see his little sister because "I want to sing to her." As the baby neared death, the mother insisted the boy get a chance to see his sister, in spite of hospital regulations against children in the ICU. So the mother escorted him in and over to the crib where the tiny baby appeared to be losing her battle to live. The little boy bent over the crib and started softly singing. "Sunshine, you are my sunshine. You make me happy when skies are gray. . . ."

Soon the baby started to respond. And he kept singing. "Sunshine, you are my sunshine. . . ." After a few minutes, miraculously, the vitals monitoring the baby indicated that her condition was stabilizing . . . and then improving. Dramatically. She turned a huge corner that day, and within a few days, she went home to a brother who called her his sunshine.

No one would assume that brother and sister always got along that well. Normal siblings don't always like each other. They learn about loyalty but also learn how to bug each other and delight in doing so. By breathing on each other or bonking each other on the head or using such endearing names as Stink Bug Breath (or much worse). They know each other's greatest vulnerabilities. But that also gives them the power to protect those vulnerabilities. At some point, they recognize they have a powerful choice: to hurt or protect those fragile parts. Will they choose loyalty?

Choosing loyalty—mature loyalty—doesn't necessarily mean choosing sameness. Siblings still may think and feel differently, but they are choosing commitment to the relationship, in spite of the differences.

The choice to loyally protect is often triggered by the threat of an outside enemy. An older brother might delight in his undisputed superiority over his little brother at home. They may wrestle and roll around on the floor like puppy dogs. But

---

Family means…
**No matter how high the hill or low the valley,
you stick together.**

---

when someone else threatens that little brother on a school playground, big brother steps in quickly to protect.

My older sister and I had our share of disagreements growing up. First over toys. (Of course, I *always* shared.) Then over who cheated on the rules to the games we played. (Of course, I *never* did!) Or who got to ride shotgun in the car. (Oldest *always* wins.) By high school, the disagreements were about clothes and whether I could ride in the car with her, because she was a senior and I was a sophomore. But I will always remember a great gesture of sister loyalty. It was the springtime of my sophomore year and the day I had tried out for cheerleader, along with three of my best friends. I was sitting in eighth-period algebra when the principal came on the public-address system.

"I have the results of the cheerleading election," he announced, "and I will read them in alphabetical order." My heart was pounding so loudly, I was sure my friends could hear it.

My last name started with a V, so I held out hope . . . until the final name was read . . . and it was not mine. I didn't make it, but my three best friends did. Soon the bell rang, and I panicked. How would I get out of this classroom and all the way down through the long, crowded hallways onto the school bus? How would I—a loser—face my friends? Numbly I stuffed my papers into my notebook and hurried toward the door, head down. Suddenly someone took my arm, and I looked up. It was my sister, who was waiting for me.

Family is . . .

**Our first experience of love that ultimately
connects us to the whole world.**

She walked with me all the way down through the crowded, noisy hallway out to the parking lot and into her car. For the life of me I don't remember a word she said. But I will never forget her gesture. She understood. She protected my vulnerability.

How do siblings learn to be loyal? From what the Bible tells us to what the experts teach us, we learn that parents play an important role in whether kids do or don't get along.

As stated earlier, they are most likely to love each other well when they are well loved. Here are a few tips.

Don't play favorites: The Bible tells the story of Joseph, the youngest child in a large family. His brothers hated him because his father favored him in so many obvious ways, like giving him a fancy, bright coat that set him apart from his siblings. Most sibling rivalry is caused by competition for parents' attention. When we play favorites or compare siblings to each other, we cause them to feel competitive and resentful toward each other. If children feel secure in our love for them, they are more likely to feel secure in showing their love for others, especially their own siblings.

Recognize the power of your words: Kids will talk to each other like they hear you talking—to them and others. Your language and tone give them permission to use the same language and tone. If they hear sarcasm, they will use sarcasm. If they hear foul words, they will use foul words, only several degrees worse. Same with positive things. Recognize and praise their loyalty to each other. "Did you teach him how to smile, Zack?" you ask the older brother when the baby smiles. Tell each child how much you love him or her. Listen to your children's words, so they expect to be heard. And don't let them use words that hurt each other.

Let them work out their differences: Kids have endless arguments about who started "IT" or whose fault "IT" is. If we refuse to referee and send them to another room to work out their differences, the solutions will be quicker and longer lasting. (Though of course we must step in to prevent them from hurting each other or teasing in hurtful ways.) One mother in a blended family of six children, ages six to sixteen, established a ritual when all the children were together. The kids were in charge of cleaning up the kitchen after dinner every night, while mom and dad went for a walk. The kids had to establish their own guidelines and work out any problems or disagreements that surfaced during that time.

Spend time together: Sounds like a no-brainer, but family together time builds family loyalty. Time together around a table. Time together in the car. Time together reading books. A young mother recalls that one of her favorite family times was when her father read a novel out loud after dinner ("and my sister and I got to play with mom's hair"). Good night and good morning together time. Hello and good-bye together time. Provide play-together time for siblings to be alone together. They learn to be better friends when there aren't always lots of other playmates around. A mom told me she avoided overscheduling her children's activities so they had time to just hang out together.

"I want my oldest to have a sense of what goes on in my youngest child's life—and to actively interact," writes a mom of four, ages ten to sixteen. "I want them to be aware of other family members' needs and affirm each other on special days or disappointing days."

We had several "no-choice family activities," which included going to each other's events, such as soccer games, horse shows, and piano recitals, at least once a season. Each child had different interests, and attending that event together as a family showed loyalty and support for that child. Those outings usually included a treat, such as dinner or dessert out, so that "no-choice family activities" didn't turn into "forced family fellowship." If dinner or dessert sounds like bribery, let me assure you that I'm all for that kind of harmless bribery. Remember, fun makes families want to be together.

Watch what they watch on television: So much meanness and sibling rivalry can come from what they see on television or videos. "They start acting like what they watch," one mom said. So watch what they watch. Less television also means more time for family interaction.

Say "I'm sorry": For children, saying "I'm sorry" often becomes just one more "parrot response" that frees them from their time-out zone after a round of sibling rivalry. Children rarely experience "sorry" on a deeper level. But this important habit builds the foundation for learning what it means to be sorry on a more mature level. One parent explained the "sorry" concept this way. She took her children into the backyard and pounded a few nails into the fence. "Every time you hurt someone, you pound another nail into a fence. You can say 'sorry' and remove the nail," she said, pulling out a nail. "But the hole is still in the fence."

Choosing to forgive is the other side of sorry and another part of choosing loyalty and commitment in a relationship. Sibling relationships are the best place to start learning this habit.

Give them models of loyalty: One father remembers how his Lebanese father used a Bible verse to teach his three boys about loyalty. He gathered the brothers together around a table. He gave them each a stick and asked if they could break their sticks. Immediately they snapped their sticks in two. Then he handed each another stick. "Now let's tie your sticks together and see if you can break them." Try as they might, the brothers could not break the bundle of three sticks. "Just remember," the father concluded. "As long as you stick together, no one can break you." ("A cord of three strands is not quickly broken," Eccles. 4:12.)

In another family, a mom pulled her older child away from an argument with a younger one. She took him to his bedroom window where he could see a hillside of lights. "Out of all those people who live out there, the ones who live in this house will be the ones who will stand by you the longest in your life," she said. "We need to stick together."

Another powerful model of loyalty is the way we get along with our own adult siblings. We can hardly imagine our little ones growing up and making choices about how much effort to put into maintaining their adult sibling relationships. But just as age and geographic location and marriage changed our own sibling relationships, the same will be true for our children. They watch how we invest ourselves in adult sibling relationships.

When our children left home for college, we wanted them to stay connected. So we gave them phone cards for calling each other. For a birthday gift, we financed a trip for the three of them to get together in San Francisco where one was going to school. Because this was their first time to be alone together without us, I emailed a joke note.

In our absence, you're bound to talk about us, so here's a couple of questions to help you get started:

Things I don't like about my mom: _____ (a very short line).

Things I love about my mom: _____
_____
_____ (a very long line).

Our oldest child, Derek, was the first to get married. At his rehearsal dinner, his two sisters proudly claimed responsibility for his sensitivity in dealing with the opposite sex. They also gave a masterful presentation of "hints for how to live with Derek." The message: siblings shape each other for life and prepare each other for all future intimate relationships in life.

When a sibling gets married, the family enters a transitional phase where everyone tries to find their place in this new family configuration. As we discussed in chapter 1, every new family member creates his or her own space in the extended family, and siblings are often confused by the new priority of relationships.

After Derek and Alex's wedding, we were seated in the airplane when Kendall began to imagine how her relationship with her brother might change. "Does this mean I can't call him and leave dumb messages on his answering machine?" she asked with tears in her eyes. I didn't really know the answer.

Another tricky adjustment period occurs when siblings start having children of their own, a season that often creates a surprising new round of sibling rivalry. It's a time when siblings get passionately protective about their own children. Here's a possible scenario.

You're all coming to the family home for Christmas. Your mom is thrilled, and so are you. Even though it means doubling and tripling up in the bedrooms and on couches, you anticipate that the visit will be like a giant slumber party, with opportunities for renewed sibling loyalty and cousin love. The first night goes pretty well, but by the second day, things start unraveling. The children are playing in the basement when one of the older, tattletale cousins comes running into the kitchen, announcing to all the adults that your three-year-old is hurting Isabella, your brother's two-year-old. You and your brother (and his wife of course) run downstairs just in time to see your daughter hit Isabella, who notices her audience and immediately begins screaming. You put your daughter in time-out, but from that moment on, your brother (and his wife of course) start shielding their pathetic wimp from your bully child.

It all goes downhill from there. The next night, your brother's four-year-old keeps waking all the other children up. "Nightmares," you hear your brother muttering, rationalizing her behavior. About four o'clock in the morning, your daughter throws up, and by the next afternoon, two others start throwing up. So your brother makes some remark about your daughter making everyone else sick. The implication makes you boiling mad, but you stuff those feelings behind a facade of "Isn't this fun?"

So much for cousin love and sibling loyalty.

But the take-heart response to such common family scenarios is the assurance that there will be a "next time." And it's bound to go better, especially as one mom decided after a similar holiday celebration: "We figured out the best family reunions happen when each family has their own motel room, a good night's sleep, and a bit of privacy." Families learn these things and keep getting together, "because we're family."

Extended Family Loyalty

Whether you've experienced a situation like that or not, loyalty with extended family cannot grow unless extended families stay connected. Grandparents and cousins matter. So do aunts and uncles and family gatherings and reunions.

We live in a culture that pulls families apart and away from each other. Children go far away from home to college and often settle down in that area. They join the military. They go off to study in a foreign country. To a mission field. To pursue other professional or educational opportunities. Staying connected becomes a long-distance challenge.

As I've already described, Lynn and I traveled around for four years while he was in the Navy. We then had a choice about where we'd settle, and we came back home. By that time we had one child with another on the way. My father had just died, and I longed to be closer to my mother, who had emphysema and was in poor health. We ended up building a house on some land next door to her house in the country, which meant I could help care for her. So our children grew up on the same hilltop in Boulder, Colorado, where I grew up. They ran back and forth on the well-worn path between our two houses, and their grandmother was a daily part of their lives until her death a few years later.

Does loyalty and commitment mean you live close to your extended family? No, but it's a choice available to many. I recently read about a Colorado family who chose to move back home to a small town in Arkansas because it cost too much to be so far away. We're not talking about the cost of travel or long-distance phone calls. We're talking about the cost of feeling disconnected. So this family gave up the shallow roots they'd established in Colorado and moved back to the deeper roots where family moments continue to shape who they are and give insights into why they are that way. For this family, the cost of this connection is priceless.

I compare that to another mother's words, which I overheard recently. She was describing the expense of getting together with extended family. The cost of airline tickets, all the packing and unpacking, to say nothing of carrying around all the emotional baggage. And giving up precious vacation time for these family get-togethers. Here's the line that's stuck with me: "So we stopped visiting."

She went on to admit that her family lost something in that solution but gained something in the way they created a new family in their new community. Many families who live far away from their extended families do create new families with friends from different generations within their community. That's a win/win solution for both the friends and the families. But new families rarely replace what original families offer. In spite of complicated relationships. In spite of differences. In spite of geographical distances, they help us know who we are because of who they are.

One friend, a young mom, admits that her relationship with her mother-in-law is strained. But what keeps her committed to that relationship is what it offers her four-year-old daughter. "In this season, the grandparent relationship is so good for both of them. That matters."

Bringing out the "grand" in grandparents: Having recently entered this new part of the extended family circle, I see how love and loyalty can grow out of these relationships. At a recent baby shower, the gifts were to be the "essentials" for this first-time mom. One young mother wrote this message to the mother-to-be: "If I could give you the most essential gift, I'd wrap up your mother, because I don't know how I could have survived the first year without mine." Grandparents can offer encouragement and help.

Long-distance relationships are a common challenge, but our high-tech world is shortening the distances. At the least, digital photos of the birthday party or trip to the pumpkin farm are sent instantly to family members around the world. At the higher end of tech-know, a growing number of families are creating their own websites to keep relatives informed of their day-to-day activities and even building cyber-windows

---

Family is…

People who know the best and worst in you but still invite you to Thanksgiving dinner.

---

into the delivery room so grandparents in Los Angeles can be "present" at the birth of their grandchild in Colorado.

I have friends on the East Coast who use their computer and a special camera to have regular, face-to-face chats with their three-year-old granddaughter on the West Coast. Their son gave them the camera and software (called iChat) for a Christmas present, and now grandparents and grandchild visit regularly, via the computer screen.

"At first we felt a bit self-conscious," Manny (the grandmother) explains, "but now we know the kind of interaction that works best during our visits with three-year-old Stella. I might show her three hats and ask which one she wants (which I send to her later) and which one she wants me and Pappa to wear. I wish we lived closer, but this keeps us connected and helps Stella feel more comfortable with us when we are together."

Keeping up with extended families doesn't have to be so tech-know. One mom writes, "We are a military family and live away from our families. So we have placemats with pictures of grandparents, aunts, uncles, and cousins so we see their faces and pray for them at dinnertime. Before Thanksgiving, we make leaves and send them to relatives and ask them to complete the sentence on the leaf and send it back. 'Grandma is thankful for _____.' We put the leaves on our Thanksgiving Tree and share their thankfulness."

Honoring our parents: Why wait until a funeral to pass on important tributes to grandparents and parents? We validate our loyalty and commitment to them when we honor them, which is a biblical commandment that has been passed down—and up—from parents to children and children to parents.

To *honor* means to attach value to a person, which can happen through many unique tributes. Creating some personal, tangible tribute, such as a scrapbook, video, or plaque, presented at a special time, blesses three generations: your parents, you, and your children. I heard about one family who adopted a stretch of highway near their parents' home in their honor (many communities offer this opportunity—and mark the section with a sign). One friend gathered photos and tributes and put together a video and book for her parents' fiftieth wedding anniversary. "I wanted them to enjoy something we did for them, not something we bought."

Another friend worked with her siblings to write a play, acted out by grandchildren at an eightieth birthday party. Families often plan a vacation or reunion for three generations where the dinner-table conversation each night is videotaped as grandparents recall family stories. One mom hosted a birthday dinner for her father-in-law and placed a piece of paper with a question under each plate. During the meal, each person asked the guest of honor these questions and others:

> Did you have any pets growing up?
>
> What is your favorite time of year and why?
>
> What kind of car did you drive when you first got your license?
>
> What was your first job?

One family honors the grandmothers their children never knew by celebrating the grandmothers' birthdays and doing something that grandparent would have enjoyed doing with the grandchild, like getting ice cream or going on a walk or hike. They talk about the grandparent on that special day.

Honoring is contagious and often triggers reverse honoring. One grandmother wrote this tribute to her daughter-in-law at Thanksgiving recently.

> It is you for whom I am most thankful. You have given our family the most unique gift ever, packaged in a beautiful baby girl. It was enough that you are the perfect soul mate for our son, but now you have done this.
>
> At MOPS (Mothers of Preschoolers), we say, "When a baby is born, a mother is born." Well, so is a grandmother. I have always loved all children, but when I saw my firstborn gazing deeply into the eyes of his firstborn, I knew this was going to be different. Life will never be the same. You have given me something no one else could give, and I am so thankful God chose you to be the mother of our first grandchild.

Grandfamilies: This word describes families that live together, several generations in one household or in neighboring houses, or families where grandparents are the heads of the household, caring for their grandchildren full-time. The number of grandfamilies is growing rapidly; about one in twelve children live with their grandparents full-time. The reasons for the growth are varied, including the increase in the number of seniors, the financial woes of young families, and the cultural influence from other countries.

Family Photos—Visual Aids of Loyalty

I'm a visual learner. Most of the population is. No wonder I like to surround myself with family photos. As I sit at my computer, I look up at a wall of photos that has grown higher and wider through the years. These pictures and many more like them are sprinkled throughout our house because family photos are visual aids of loyalty and commitment. You know how good you feel if you walk into someone's house and see your picture displayed on their refrigerator door or in a frame on a shelf? That's how kids feel when they see their pictures around the house.

Our kids grew up seeing pictures of themselves with their arms around each other in front of the Christmas tree, jump-

---

**"Write down for the coming generation
what the Lord has done,
so that people not yet born will praise him."**
~ Psalm 102:18 GNT

---

ing into the swimming pool on summer vacations, on family hikes. These pictures have been magnet-ed to the refrigerator door and stuck in frames on the kitchen counters, window-sills, shelves, and walls all over the house. I know the mini-malist look is in (less is more; uncluttered is best), and I've tried to clean up my photo act, but photos matter to me. In addition to what is seen, I've got hundreds more stashed in drawers and bulging photo albums, and more recently, saved inside our computer. I'm probably a photo junkie.

Family photos fill our hearts with messages of love and loyalty. Remember that hole of longing I described in the chapter on love? It's that love-hungry place within all of us that gets filled up, teaspoonful by teaspoonful. Family photos pour love into that place of longing by the bucketsful. How? By refreshing our good memories. We take pictures of happy times. Family milestones and celebrations. The Kodak moments of our lives. And the more we see these pictures, the more those reminders fill us up.

Christmas cards matter in the same way in our family. I'm motivated to keep taking and sending unique family-photo greeting cards each year because each year's card summarizes what mattered most in our family that year. A new baby. Our move into a new house. Another baby. Good news and not-so-good news is woven into each card. Each year I save a card for each child, and someday I will make a family

---

"Families stick together in all kinds of trouble."
~ Proverbs 17:17 Message

Christmas card album for each of them. Just like my mother did for me.

From where I'm sitting I can see one of my favorite family photos. It's me and my two younger brothers and older sister, taken at a recent family wedding. There we are, all dressed up, striking one of the same goofy poses we always did as children. Taped to the bottom of the picture is a quote I found somewhere: "Be kind to your siblings. They're your best link to your past and the people most likely to stick with you in the future."

That's the message of family loyalty. We learn it, and then we learn it is a choice, in the midst of messy and complicated issues. It demands sacrifice for the common good. And for-giveness. Here's my bias: it's worth it. When we choose loy-alty, we choose commitment to those who are most likely to stick with us in the future.

Wonderings

1. What does "family loyalty" mean to you?
2. What do you do (that you don't always feel like doing) "because we're family"?
3. I offered several ways for parents to build sibling loyalty (pages 129–31), including

   Don't play favorites.

   Recognize the power of your words.

   Let them work out their differences.

   Say "I'm sorry."

   Which of these four is easiest for you? Why? Which is your greatest challenge? Why?
4. Honoring your parents blesses three generations. Here are some questions to help you think of ways to honor your parents.

   What did my parents do right in my life? (We usually answer the opposite question: what did my parents do wrong?)

   What sacrifices did my parents make for me?

   How did they model family loyalty?

   How could you uniquely honor your parents for these legacies?

7

Growth

Growing Keeps Us Healthy

On the first night of our family vacation in the Colorado mountains, we stopped at a small dude ranch with a few rustic cabins and a great swimming pool tucked into the valley between two sheer canyon walls. As we strolled back to our cabin after dinner in the dining hall, we saw that no one was in the pool. So we changed into our suits and jumped into the cool water in the gathering darkness. Soon, a bright full moon peaked over the canyon wall, bathing our idyllic moment in golden light as we splashed around the pool. Even the kids, ages five, eight, and ten, seemed mesmerized.

It was one of those near-perfect family moments. Gone were the memories of earlier in the day in the car when they bickered and bugged each other and I didn't like any of them.

"Freeze!" I wanted to yell. "Everyone stay just as you are. Nobody change! Nobody grow!"

That's a silly wish, of course. We can't freeze our family in those near-perfect moments; we can't stay in a swimming pool for the rest of our lives. We'd surely freeze, all right, but life doesn't "freeze," and growing is good. Growing means we're healthy. Not growing is bad. Not growing means we're not really living.

Besides, growing doesn't come in those near-perfect, idyllic, swimming-pool moments. It comes more often in the car, when everyone's bugging each other and we know we have to grin and bear it and get along. Growing is what we get when we don't get what we want. Growing happens when we push through a challenge, as individuals and as a family.

In a family, two kinds of growth matter. Outside growth, or physical growth. And inside growth, which is character growth.

In the beginning, we focus more on physical growth. From the moment our first child was born, I was concerned about his growth. Is he eating enough and gaining enough weight? Or too much? At his regular checkups, the nurse ceremoniously weighed and measured him, and later, the pediatrician announced where he fell on some arbitrary scale of all the babies in the whole wide world: "He's in the eightieth percentile in height and sixtieth percentile in weight." As moms, we either feel guilty or good about how our baby compares to the world of other babies. Why? Because growing is good. Growing means healthy.

We continue to watch our children grow physically. We might chart their growth at home with smudgy marks on the laundry-room door. We watch their out-growth, measured by piles of outgrown clothes and shoes. Outgrown car seats, cribs, toys, and books. We're alternately awed by the speed of their growth and then stunned by its slowness. We want them to slow down or speed up and get on to the next stage. Yet, when we finally give those outgrown items away or sell them at a garage sale, we mark a different kind of bittersweet growth spot in our family. No reason to save those hand-me-downs because there will be no more babies.

Growth is about more than the physical process of growing bigger or older or growing a larger family. Growth that matters most is about inside growth. Growing more responsible. Growing more patient. Growing less critical. Growing more assertive. Growing toward maturity by finding answers to those lifelong questions about who I am and where I'm going in life and how I'm going to get there. A healthy family is a growing family, where each person is encouraged to grow toward their own answers to those questions.

Because a healthy family is a growing family, our challenge is to create an environment where individuals grow both separately and together, finding balance between the two. A family that grows together but not individually can become enmeshed and codependent. Family members resist thinking for themselves; instead, they value sameness and groupthink as intimacy. Individuals have fuzzy edges and blurry boundaries. They don't know where one person stops and the other begins. They own each other's problems, which means no one learns to take responsibility for themselves.

A healthy family is a growing family made up of individuals who are not totally independent or codependent but interdependent, counting on each other for love and support while growing individually. This family can sit around a dinner table and feel safe expressing their differing opinions.

Hold On Lightly . . . Not Too Tightly

The way to grow a healthy family is grow an openhanded attitude about letting go and trusting God who provides what we need. A healthy family has an attitude that holds each other lightly, not too tightly.

We have a visual aid at our house that reminds me of that attitude. It's a sculpture displayed on top of a bookcase in the most prominent spot in our kitchen–family room area. It would be one of the first things I'd grab if the house caught fire. Let me tell you the story behind that piece of art.

When our children were babies, I recognized that one of my challenges in life would be learning to let go. I am that fix-it mom who likes to plan the day. Plan the week. Plan our children's lives, everything from activities to car pools to what they have for snacks. No wonder I think I can also fix their problems and protect them from pain. Create their solutions. This instinct means I'm apt to hold on too tightly. In the name of love.

Years ago, I read a Bible story about a father who probably felt the same way. His name was Abraham, and he and his wife were old when their baby boy was born. They named him Isaac. He was the child they had so longed for, and the boy quickly became the treasure of his father's heart. Did Abraham begin to treasure Isaac more than he trusted God? Did he begin to hold on too tightly?

I know that temptation. The more we value something, the more tightly we wrap our fingers around it. People put their valuable jewelry in safe-deposit boxes. They protect their homes with costly alarm systems. We hold our children more tightly and closer to our sphere of control. When I do this, am I treasuring my child more than trusting God?

In this Bible story, God tells Abraham to take Isaac up Mt. Moriah and surrender him to God in that place. Abraham responds in obedience, but surely that three-day trek to reach the top of that mountain with his son must have been the longest, hardest journey of this father's life. It was a journey toward surrendering the treasure of his heart to

Loving and Letting Go

Loving and letting go is a lifelong challenge for parents. It requires both tough and tender choices. Along the way, we're helped by keeping our goals in mind. Here are some guidelines that keep the process in perspective:

1. Loving and letting go is one of the most critical responsibilities of parenting that meets a child's greatest need: to grow toward healthy independence.

2. Letting go is a lifelong process that starts the moment the umbilical cord is cut at birth and continues in little steps and starts, moment by moment, as a child grows up.

3. Letting go demands a gradual change in the way we express our love for our children, from total control in infancy to no control at maturity. The goal is to take care of them until they can take care of themselves.

4. Letting go is a process marked by the balanced, orderly granting of freedom and responsibility, year by year, as the child grows up.

5. Letting go means we encourage and celebrate (not thwart) our children's appropriate steps of independence. Their success is our success.

God. The description of the uphill journey reminds me of so many journeys I have taken as a mother, to reach a place of surrender and letting go. In trust.

When Derek was diagnosed diabetic at age nine, I faced a crisis in my heart. I couldn't fix this problem. There was no cure. The doctor could not hand me a prescription that would make this go away. Nor could he give me any assurance that Derek wouldn't face some of the critical, life-threatening problems that diabetics face. I had a choice. To hold on more tightly and try to control every possible remaining life circumstance that might affect him and our whole family—or let go and surrender his life to God, trusting that God would control his circumstances and provide what he and the rest of us need most . . . even if we face our worst fears.

One way would confine Derek to grow according to my plan; the other would allow him to grow according to God's plan, which might well be different from mine. I'll never forget the long, slow journey of my heart toward surrender. But Abraham showed me the way. His story shows that when we surrender the treasures of our hearts to God, he gives us the peace and comfort of knowing that he is in control. Even when or if we face the unexpected or unimaginable.

The sculpture on the shelf in our home is my daily reminder of this truth. It shows Abraham, holding up his son Isaac in a gesture of surrender. The joy on Abraham's face reflects this father's total, loving delight in Isaac. The boy's face mirrors the same joy. The incredible beauty of the piece is the way the father holds his son—with his hands open—symbolic of his surrender of this treasure of his heart.

Lynn surprised me with this sculpture on my birthday years ago. Ever since, its presence in our home reminds me that I need to have this attitude of surrender for each member of our family. We let go of each other in order to allow God to grow us in his way. We allow the baby of the family to grow out of her role as the funny family mascot. We respect the fiercely independent child's need for more privacy. We're reminded to hold on lightly . . . not too tightly.

So how do we live out this attitude in our families?

Guess what? It starts with us and the attitudes we have about our own personal growth. Do we hold ourselves lightly or tightly when it comes to growing? Do we have an attitude of trust as we open ourselves up to a growth plan that stretches us? Are we growing in several different areas?

How are you growing?

Mom Growth

No doubt, you are busy growing your children (who will be measured again soon on that growth chart at the pediatrician's office) and meeting their needs (keeping them in clothes that fit, stimulating their brains with good books and interesting experiences, arranging carpools or day care and activity schedules). Whew! No wonder you hardly have time to consider that you too have needs for physical, emotional, spiritual, and intellectual growth.

Let's take a growth check. Don't worry. This doesn't measure and give you a ranking in comparison to all the other mothers in the whole wide world! And your results won't be publicly announced and recorded like at the pediatrician's office. This is about personal growth, so your answers remain personal.

How are you different this year than a year ago at this time? Let's narrow that question to a few specific areas of your life, spiritually or in mothering, for instance. Do you see progress toward a goal? I confess that I feel discouraged as I try to answer these questions. Why aren't I a better mother who chooses to do the right thing more often? Or how come I still can't quickly find Colossians in a Bible without side tabs?

I look at the bookcases in our house, filled with titles I've read in different seasons. Books on marriage and family and personal growth that I devoured when our kids were preschoolers. "Scary mommy books" I read when they were in grade school that made me fear I'd already hopelessly messed them up. Then there were books about letting go, including the two I even wrote on the subject. Did all that reading and writing help me grow or make me better? Did I retain any of that knowledge or apply it? I'm thankful that I underlined or highlighted some text in most of them, because at least that proves I read them.

Then I see examples of the person I don't want to be and wonder if I've made any progress toward the person I want to be. I don't want to be like the nagging wife I watched at the airport who kept harping at her husband because their plane was delayed and she wanted him to do something about it. I don't want to be like the mom at the restaurant who kept criticizing her preschool-aged son for acting like a child. I don't want to nag or criticize like that. Am I making any progress toward such a goal?

Yes! Mothering is growing us, and we are all making progress. One of the problems is that we're all pretty hard on ourselves when it comes to self-evaluations. We're apt to hold ourselves tightly, with fists clenched closed instead of with an openness to recognize and accept how God is growing us.

There's a saying: "You aren't yet the woman God wants you to be, but you also aren't the woman you used to be." You are growing, and you can be encouraged by opening your eyes to the visible progress you're making in the sometimes-invisible process of growing. In parenting, consider what you didn't know with your first child. You probably felt inadequate at times, confused and overwhelmed at the responsibility of raising a child. I'll bet that if you have more than one child, you knew much more with your second child. Consider the skills you are developing in mothering: research skills, leadership skills, critical-thinking skills. As women, we have an innate ability to weave what we learn into all our life experiences. Mothering grows us!

Yet mothering is not our only role, and we're not yet the women God desires us to be. We need to grow in other areas of our lives. Beyond where we are in our faith ... marriage ... friendships ... physical fitness ... or professional skills ... to name just a few.

We're not going to be measured and compared to the whole wide world of growing women, but we can measure ourselves, using these prescriptive suggestions for growing.

Be teachable: "You just can't change me," my mother sometimes said, which made me both mad and sad. Our willingness to keep learning means allowing others to change us.

I hope I allow my children to change me—along with my husband and my friend who tells me the truth and my life circumstances that don't always turn out the way I want. Just because we're grown-up, we're not done growing. Even Michelangelo at age eighty-seven was quoted as saying, "*Ancoro imparo*," which means, "I am still learning." After all he had already accomplished in his life, his attitude was that there was still more to learn and discover! The Bible talks about being hard-hearted and stiff-necked, attitudes that keep us from growing. A teachable spirit opens us up to growth—and being teachable makes us better teachers!

Create your own personal growth plan: I recently had my annual evaluation at work, which pointed out my need to grow my technical skills. (Duh! I knew that but had no plan . . . until now . . . when I have a computer tutorial CD on my desk, just waiting for me.)

Where do you want to grow? Define some areas in your life where you'd like to grow. Spiritually? Better self care? Listening skills? If you can't think of any, ask your family where

---

Family means . . .

Never feeling alone, no matter how far away you are.

---

you need to grow. (That takes courage and vulnerability! But both are good character qualities to grow, so you're already on your way!) Evaluations from other people can motivate us to get specific about our growth plan.

Hang out with people who stretch you: I recently spent an evening with girlfriends, exchanging stories about our children and the challenges of mothering. One friend perfectly mimicked the inappropriate sounds and words that come out of her young sons' mouths at the dinner table. Another gave a description of the guilt trips people send her on because she is a working mother. Another described how she tried to control her anger when her son threw up in church after taking his first communion. I almost threw up laughing at her descriptions! Their contagious humor exercised mine, knocking it up a notch. Do you spend time with people who are different from you, people who stretch your thinking on parenting issues, politics, or spiritual issues? Or people who exercise your sense of humor? Stretching is good for us.

Take risks: Lots of moms tell me they want to write. "Why don't you?" I ask. "I'm afraid I can't," is often the answer. The fear of failure keeps us from growing, but failing doesn't make us failures. It grows us. If you want to write, buy a book on writing, attend a writer's workshop, find a topic you feel passionate about, and start writing! Be willing to take a risk and step into a less-than-comfortable place. Why not try public speaking. Writing. Taking on a leadership role. Sharing your faith!

My daughter-in-law recently set a physical goal of doing a minitriathlon to celebrate her thirtieth birthday. Swimming a long way in a murky lake is not her idea of fun, so pursuing the goal stretched her way outside her comfort zone, but she did it! You've probably heard this saying: when you're in a comfort zone, you're not in a growth zone; when you're in a growth zone, you're not in a comfort zone.

Know when to ask for help: At work recently, I had trouble filling out an Excel report on the computer. The more frustrated I got, the more I pounded away on the keys, and the more boxes on the screen disappeared. But I didn't want to ask for help. Why? Because I didn't want to appear helpless. Why do we think we're better or more godly if we do life on our own and hesitate to ask others for help? Is it because we don't want to seem incapable or dumb? Or dependent instead of independent?

God created us to be dependent upon others. Recognizing our needs and dependency is critical to growing relationships and growing a healthy family. Whether it's help in dealing with a child or advice in dealing with a financial problem, asking for help is a response of strength, not weakness. It's a wise choice and one of the greatest lessons we can pass on to our children.

Turn crisis into opportunity: Many of our passions and pursuits grow out of our family situations, especially our challenges. A mother with a special-needs child challenges and changes the school system's program for children like hers. A mother with an adopted child from China helps other families find their way through the foreign-adoption process. A mom with a diabetic child establishes a website for other parents with diabetic children. A mom who had a baby at age seventeen writes a book for other teenage moms. These moms grow by turning a crisis into an opportunity.

If we hold ourselves lightly, not too tightly, we open ourselves to a lifelong process of growing, which is contagious. Our desire for growth sparks the same desire in those around us.

Family Proverbs from The Message

We find wisdom in the book of Proverbs in the Bible. Wisdom means applying what we know in whatever circumstances we find ourselves in. Wisdom helps us grow as a family!

Intelligent children listen to their parents; foolish children do their own thing. 13:1

Knowing what is right is like deep water in the heart; a wise person draws from the well within. 20:5

God-loyal people, living honest lives, make it much easier for their children. 20:7

Watch your words and hold your tongue; you'll save yourself a lot of grief. 21:23

If you fall to pieces in a crisis, there wasn't much to you in the first place. 24:10

Playing favorites is always a bad thing; you can do great harm in seemingly harmless ways. 28:21

Don't curse your father or fail to bless your mother. 30:11

Family Growth

How do you make room for family growth? Earlier we said the key to family growth is creating an environment where people are encouraged to grow both separately and together. Holding on to each other lightly, not too tightly. Allowing individuals to grow in their own direction, even when it is not "our direction." Carl Jung once said, "Nothing affects the life of a child so much as the unlived life of its parent."

Healthy growth means allowing individuals to be uniquely themselves within the context of a single family. When our kids were young and we came together at mealtime, we had one child who loved sports and came running to the table wearing sweatbands on his head and wrists; another who loved animals and would have liked to turn dinnertime into show-and-tell time by bringing her hamsters and rabbits to the table; and one who mostly knew what she *didn't* like and sat in her high chair yelling really loud, just to be heard. Dinnertime was often a time of chaos, but the important part of that chaos was weaving those separate parts together around a single table.

Here's what I've learned about growing separately but together as a family.

Expect and embrace change: One thing for sure, those adorable little babies will grow up. From personal experience I can tell you that little boy throwing a tantrum because of a disagreement at age two will be taller than you and disagreeing with some political viewpoint at age sixteen. (He may also have a shaved head and double earrings!) The daughter who insists on dressing herself at age four (looking silly in her layered, mismatched outfits) will be borrowing your clothes and telling you how to dress at age fourteen. That's about the time I became my daughters' personal rehabilitation project.

In the life journey of a family, everybody will grow and change the ways they think and act, which requires everyone else to embrace and adjust to those changes! We can't parent a twelve-year-old the same way we parent a two-year-old. A sister has to respect her older brother's relationship with a girlfriend. We have to constantly adjust to our children's growth from dependence to independence, and they have to embrace the same changes in each other. We're connected with a rubber-band kind of love, strong enough to hold us together but stretchy enough to embrace the expected changes.

Give lots of wiggle room: There's a saying, "If the shoe fits, you're not allowing for growth." How true. When we buy shoes for our kids, we don't want the shoes to fit snugly. We want them to offer wiggle room for the expected growth. Same with families.

Children need increasing amounts of wiggle room as they move from dependence to independence. When they are preschoolers, we don't give too much wiggle room. In their season of total dependency, we pretty much control their choices and their environment: what they eat and when they eat it; what they wear; where they sleep. (Notice I did not say "*when* they sleep . . ." because who can *control* a baby's sleep?)

As they grow, we give more wiggle room, which is hard for some parents who get used to controlling their children's environment and choices. This is the season when we have to start letting go and allow our children to experience the consequences of their choices.

I've already admitted that I'm a fix-it mom who was always tempted to overprotect our children. I didn't like to see them making poor choices, and I certainly didn't like waiting around and watching them endure the consequences while they learned a lesson. While the six-year-old learned how to handle the mean kid on the soccer team. While the ten-year-old learned to ask the teacher for help when she didn't understand. I was tempted to rush in and fix those problems, stepping in between the child and the lesson. But as kids grow up, they need more and more wiggle room. More space to grow.

By the time our children reached their senior year in high school, we gave them even more wiggle room. After all, they were nearly ready to face life beyond our home, on a college campus or in the working world, where we hoped they would stand strong in the midst of all the temptations they'd face. We too needed wiggle room in this season, as we prepared ourselves for their independence. As parents, our goal is to work ourselves out of a job, and by the time our kids leave home, at maybe age eighteen, we should not be controlling their choices. Our aim is to reach a mutually satisfying adult-to-adult relationship of interdependence with our children, based on the relationship of respect we've built through the years.

Learn to work through conflict together: Let's be real. People get mad at each other, even in the closest families. One of the most important ingredients of a healthy family is learning to work through conflicts. In some families, people yell their way through conflicts. In other families, people stuff their feelings, assuming "good families" don't argue or ever raise their voices.

Healthy families fall in the middle of these two extremes, learning to work through conflicts with loving honesty. Even young children have to learn to express their frustrations. "I want my preschoolers to know that family is a safe place to express their feelings without fear of being punished," a friend told me. They also have to see parents work through their frustrations.

When it comes to frustration or conflict in a family, here's a good first question to ask: "Is this your problem or my problem or our problem?" In most conflicts, it's *our* problem. Sometimes anger will keep you from dealing well with the conflict, so "time out" has to be taken before discussing the problem. Then the key is to use "I" messages, which is the honest way to address the issue. Instead of, "You make me feel dumb when you don't listen to my opinion," say, "I feel dumb when you don't even listen to my opinion." Try to listen to each other well when confronting an issue, without being defensive. Remember that the goal is to restore the relationship when confronting an issue. Attack the problem, not the person.

Practice forgiving each other: Forgiving is more than saying sorry, though with children it starts with the habit of saying, "I'm sorry." It means not keeping score and not holding grudges. It means choosing not to bring up the incident over and over and choosing to move forward beyond the issue. It means making that choice again and again.

Embrace mistakes: We all make mistakes. We learn how to do it right by doing it wrong. Family is the place where we learn how to learn from our mistakes.

Talk. Talk. Talk: Taking time to talk and listen to each other, especially about seemingly insignificant things, establishes a pattern. If we don't talk to our kids about stuff that doesn't matter, they're not likely to talk to us about stuff that does. Small talk leads to bigger talk.

Grow through crisis: We all face crises in life, those times when something happens that affects the whole family. The loss of a job, a move, diagnosis of a serious health problem, a death, broken relationships, divorce. Children learn to handle adversity as they watch adults pick up the broken pieces. Do they see that we believe good things can grow out of hard things? Do we have hope?

In our family, Derek's diabetes at age nine felt like a family crisis. The diagnosis explained his sudden critical illness as we rushed to the hospital early in the morning of his sister Lindsay's eighth birthday. That timing deepened the impact of the family crisis. How would we carry on with her slumber-party birthday with Derek in the hospital? We managed, somewhat poorly, with a plan that fell far short of her birthday dream. Twenty years later, on Lindsay's twenty-eighth birthday, Derek marked the milestone of living well with diabetes by climbing a fourteen-thousand-foot peak in Colorado with some buddies. That night, we gave Lindsay back her eighth birthday party, a great, playful celebration with balloons and hats and games like Pin the Tail on the Donkey.

Through family crisis, we learn to separate what we can and can't control. We do our best with what is humanly possible and lift the impossible to God in prayer. It's summed up in Reinhold Niebuhr's familiar prayer:

> God, grant me the serenity to accept the things I cannot change,
> The courage to change the things I can,
> And the wisdom to know the difference.

And we try to find the hope in the difficult situations.

Enlarge your family circle: This is the way we reach beyond our family circle with an awareness of the larger world. Without realizing it, families sometimes close ranks, excluding rather than welcoming others into the family circle. A friend told me she was still learning the necessary flexibility of this family quality. At her son's high school graduation lunch recently, two of his friends showed up for the family celebration. They had nowhere else to go. So the family pulled up a couple of extra chairs. During the meal, several more showed up. She had to ask herself, "What's more important here—having our own family celebration with enough food to eat, or being a family that welcomes others?" She knew the answer as they scoured the house for more chairs.

We add chairs and enlarge our circle to welcome new friends and in-laws and adopted grandparents and foreign students or the church intern who needs a place to sleep. We resist the kind of rigid edges that exclude people; instead we soften the edges and widen our circle, not only so that family members can come and go freely, but so that they can leave and return and bring others with them.

Celebrate Growth!

Think of the ways we celebrate steps of growth in our families. We squeal and clap with delight at a baby's first steps. We let the tooth fairy leave something special that rewards the loss of baby teeth. We put children's foot- or handprints in the wet cement on the back patio. We take pictures and videos of our children on every birthday, first day of school, graduation, and all the other times they are doing something that matters to them and to us. We hardly need a parenting manual to tell us to celebrate these milestone moments in our families.

Baby books are another way we celebrate children's growth. Some moms are faithful to record all their baby's "firsts" in the appropriate blanks in some sweet pink or blue book. First smile. First time to turn over. First word. First steps. I always intended to do this. Almost since birth, each child has had a big plastic box I keep on a shelf above my desk. I started tossing stuff in those boxes, everything from the little bracelet that identified each of them in the hospital nursery to their high school and college graduation pictures. I figured someday I would enjoy putting their baby books together when I had more time. That "someday" has never come, and now my daughter Lindsay and her husband, Jeff, are expecting their first child in a few months. She recently told me that her mother-in-law had just given her Jeff's baby book, which neatly chronicled all his "firsts."

That conversation sent me straight to Lindsay's big plastic box. After I removed five daggers of guilt from my heart, I started digging for little scraps of paper where I might have recorded a few of her "firsts." I must have assumed that I'd never forget those "firsts" or that nobody would care, because I found none. But somebody does care. Lindsay cares. She'd like to compare them to her baby's "firsts." Celebrating growth—by recording important milestones—matters.

Minimilestones are tucked into little everyday moments, unique to every family. One mother wrote about those holy moments that celebrate her child's growth while also making her feel better as a mom. "I feel better the moment Patrick, my two-year-old autistic son, wakes me by touching my face and saying 'Up!' Why? Because only a few weeks ago, he couldn't

---

Family is . . .
The heartbeat of your life.

---

say a word. I feel better when my four-year-old son, Diego, yells out to his older brother as he leaves for school, 'I love you, Douglas!' Why? Because last week they couldn't stand each other. . . . In these moments my children remind me that no matter how much I have done wrong, God helped me do something right."

Family funerals can also serve as meaningful celebrations of growth, because they offer an opportunity to recall legacies that will live on. All three of our children spoke at their grandfather's funeral a few years ago, describing the ways his passions and character will continue to impact their lives.

Many parents are unsure whether to take children to a funeral, but after lots of children attended Lynn's parents' funerals, I can assure you that children offer an ongoing sense of hope with their presence.

Weddings are one of a family's most festive growth markers. The significance of the celebration ripples out across the generations. The bride and groom are central of course, but their marriage marks an important change-point in their parents' lives and enlarges the family circle by uniting two sometimes-very-different extended families. At my own wedding, I remember looking around at the gathering of friends and relatives, stunned that they would come from as far away as New York City and Seattle to celebrate with us in Colorado.

My youngest daughter, Kendall, was the first of our two daughters to get married, and shortly after her engagement, I began to realize how a wedding can trigger some complicated, healthy growth in a family. Since I was new to this mother-of-the-bride role, I took advice from friends more seasoned in the role who told me that I needed to let the bride and groom do most of the planning. "In fact," one friend advised, "it's best if you have simply no opinion."

I did just fine with cake flavors and the color of the bridesmaids' dresses and choices about flowers and music. But I surprised myself with the passion I felt about one element of the ceremony: the lighting of the unity candle, which symbolizes the couple's two lives becoming one. This is how the ritual goes: at the start of the ceremony, the mothers of the bride and groom light two separate candles representing the bride and groom. Then, after repeating their vows, the bride and groom take the two candles and together light the single unity candle. Now here's the choice: do you blow out the two separate candles—or leave them burning? The pastor said it's done both ways, but I suddenly couldn't stand the thought of Kendall blowing her own candle out.

"Don't," I begged in a vulnerable moment one night as she and I sat together at the kitchen counter going over some of the wedding details. "You don't snuff out the person you are when you get married," I said, holding back the unspoken plea, "You don't snuff out the family you've come from."

Kendall looked at me, confused by the emotion in my voice. "I'll talk to David," she responded, an increasingly familiar (and appropriate) answer.

Up until the wedding, I thought about those silly candles and realized I might be taking the symbolism a bit too far. But my feelings reminded me that accepting growth and change is part of a family's lifelong challenge. We hold on loosely,

---

"We must never be content not to grow for if you are not growing more, you are growing less—if the light is not increasing, darkness is encroaching."
~ George MacDonald,
nineteenth-century Scottish minister

---

not too tightly, and keep learning to let go as they make their own choices.

Surely you must wonder—what did Kendall and David do with their candles on their wedding day? I confess that I was tempted to substitute those trick candles that reignite even after you blow them out, just in case. I took a deep breath as together they lighted their unity candle, set their burning candles back into the holders—and didn't blow them out.

As this newly married couple walked down the aisle, the flames on those three candles grew brighter, as they should when the family circle grows bigger.

Growing individually and growing together keeps a family healthy through the seasons of life. It means embracing change and celebrating the results that say, "Wow! Look at how we're growing!"

Wonderings

Mom Growth

1. In what areas of your life do you want to grow in the next year? What will you do specifically to grow closer to your goal?
2. Think of a major event in your life in the last year. In what ways did you grow through that experience?
3. Think of a place that inspires you to reflect upon your personal growth. (A chair in your living room, a quiet corner of your community library, a church chapel or park.) When's the last time you put yourself in that spot? How could you put yourself there more often?

Family Growth

4. What are you doing this year to help your child(ren) grow from dependence to independence? How are you treating your child differently today than you did two years ago?
5. Character traits include honesty, compassion, patience, and perseverance, to name a few. What DVDs or books have you enjoyed as a family that promote character growth? (One of my personal favorites is the classic *The Little Engine That Could*.)
6. There's a story about a little boy who fell out of bed one night. "What happened?" his mother asked anxiously. "I guess I stayed too close to where I got in," he answered. What does this mean about growth? How does it apply to the growth of your family?

21 Practical Parenting Tips

1. Let your children know you love them, no matter what.
2. Help them find something they feel good about being good at.
3. Keep rules to a minimum. Keep the main thing the main thing.
4. Loosen, don't tighten, the reins as they grow.
5. Let them be kids.
6. Encourage them to pursue their dreams, not your expectations.
7. Don't nag.
8. Teach them how to think, not what to think.
9. Allow them to experience the consequences of their choices.
10. Enlarge their circles and allow others to fill in the spaces you can't always fill.
11. Don't regularly do for them what they can do for themselves.
12. Let them fight their own battles.
13. Treat them with respect. Let them have and voice their own opinions.
14. Give them your confidence, not your worries.
15. Lighten up. Have fun together.
16. Be real. Admit your mistakes. Apologize when necessary.
17. Find common ground.
18. Make the most of life's irretrievable moments.
19. Pray for them. Unceasingly.
20. Trust God.
21. Remember, it is never too late to make an eternal difference in the lives of your children. Start from where you are . . . today.

8

Faith

Faith Lights Our Way Home

I sank down in seat 24A, stuffed my carry-on bag under the seat in front of me, and gazed out the airplane window into the dark night. After an exhausting two-day conference in Dallas, I just wanted to get home.

I checked my watch and did the math. My plane was due to land in Denver about 9:30 p.m. With any luck, I'd be able to find my car in the lot and be home in Boulder by 11:00. In spite of the snow in the forecast.

Ahhhhh . . . home . . . where even the familiar click of the garage-door opener welcomes me to the place where I belong. As the plane took off, I closed my eyes. . . .

Scratch the luck. Just as we began our descent, the pilot updated the weather report. A fierce, fast-moving storm was dumping heavy snow in Denver, and we would be landing in near-blizzard conditions.

Sure enough. As the plane touched down, huge flakes swirled around the windows, and the pilot warned us about the wind and cold temperatures.

No joke.

By the time I made my way through the terminal, I heard the announcement that the airport was closing down. I hurried out the doors to the parking lot, where icy, blowing flakes stung my face. And the cars, now buried under the heavy snow, looked like rows of identical, giant snowballs.

"Oh no," I groaned and then remembered how clicking my key not only unlocks my car doors, it flashes the taillights. "Light, baby, light," I coaxed the row of cars in the area where I thought mine was parked. Soon, several cars down, I saw a faint pink light flickering through the snow.

"Thank you, Lord," I murmured.

I brushed the cementlike snow off the windows and backed out, thankful for four-wheel drive. Just as I headed for the airport exit, all the streetlights went off. In the darkness and swirling snow, I felt like I'd totally lost my way. I inched along, not even sure where the road was. Suddenly another car emerged out of the darkness and slowly passed me, as if to say, "I know the way. Follow my taillights." And I did. For the next two hours, as I crept through the dark and snowy night, I found and followed the taillights of other cars in front of me.

They lighted my way home.

Faith is like that light in our lives. It lights our way in dark places. It points us in the right direction. It helps us make right choices. Faith lights our pathway home to God's presence.

Home for me—in the earthly setting of time and place—is a house on a plot of land on a hilltop in Boulder where my family has lived for nearly three generations. I used to joke with our children, as they grew up, that they could go off on their worldly adventures, but when they got married and started having children of their own, they needed to come home. "And home," I always told them, "is where your mom lives." (I probably should add that they always rolled their eyes in response, until they got totally numb to such talk, which even their dad called "drivel.")

In the spiritual sense, home is much bigger. Today, it is the place where we are nestled safely and securely in God's hand. Tomorrow, home is the place where we will live eternally with him.

Faith lights the way home—for today and tomorrow.

Faith Matters

People who know about healthy families tell us that faith matters in families. Doctors, teachers, and counselors agree. Faith strengthens families. It puts broken relationships back together; it gives us hope beyond our circumstances; it helps us love unlovely people; it gives meaning and purpose to our lives. Naturally we want faith-full families, but how do we reach that result? Faith-full families begin with personal faith. Yours and mine. We can't pass on something that we ourselves don't have.

I didn't really know what faith meant when I was growing up. I thought I had it because my family went to church once in a while. At least we didn't *never* go, like some people I knew. We'd attend an Easter Sunrise or Christmas Eve service. We also said grace ... at least once a year at Thanksgiving. And I knew who Jesus was ... the little papier-mâché baby in the manger that we got out every Christmas and put on a table, like a decoration.

What turned me toward faith in God was that longing for love in my heart. Starting in high school, I couldn't find anything that would satisfy that longing within me. A mother's love meets that longing when we're young, but as we grow up, we realize that even mothers aren't perfect. They can hurt our feelings or let us down or break a promise. Accepting this reality represents an important step of growth, especially as we build more lasting relationships with other real and imperfect people.

High school was a time of longing for something I couldn't find. A best friend? She wasn't consistent. A boyfriend? He didn't stick around. Success? I lost that cheerleading election, even though my mother had always promised I could be anything I wanted to be if I just tried hard enough. I tried harder than anyone else I knew, and I failed. Life sometimes hurt in high school, and my longings deepened.

One boy who seemed different from the rest went to

Family means…
Being loved when you least deserve it.

---

church. So I started going to church, and the experience felt good. Today I can't remember anything specific I learned, but I kept going, long after that boy disappeared. I even decided to join the church and took a class. But on the day that prospective members were to stand up and confess their faith, I was sick. The truth is that I didn't feel good that day because I wasn't sure what it meant to "confess my faith." I must have slipped through the cracks, because I received a certificate of membership anyway. I liked the feeling of belonging and began to slowly grow in my knowledge of the Bible.

While in college, I met and fell in love with Lynn, and we started attending that church together. We liked the pastor, and when we got engaged and then married, he performed the ceremony. When we started a family, he baptized all three of our babies. When I experienced the roller-coaster ride of emotional ups and downs as a mother of three children, I found encouragement from this pastor and friends, people who could light my way.

When our children were young, I signed up for a women's Bible study that offered free child care. To be honest, I might have been more excited about the child care than about starting my first Bible study. But it was during that class that faith began to make sense to me. I already believed what I was learning, but I was putting the pieces together in a more meaningful way. It was a slow process of God's truth lighting the way.

Faith Lights the Way

Some people come to faith in an instant . . . a single, dramatic moment of clarity, like flipping the light switch on in a dark room. Immediately the room is brightly illuminated. I wish I had a dramatic story like that. My process was more like night turning into day. I went to bed, and it was dark outside. When I woke up, it was light. I knew I was living in a new day, but I do not know the exact moment that night turned into day. Even if I had stayed up all night, I would not have known that exact moment.

With the dawn of a new day, light slowly overtakes the darkness, illuminating the night out of all the nooks and crannies of the landscape. That's how it had been for me all those years since I started going to church in high school. The more I learned about Jesus, the more he kept illuminating the dark places of longing in my heart. Slowly I began to understand the God-hunger in my heart—that God satisfies through a personal relationship with his son Jesus—who fills those longing places with his love.

By the time I went to that Bible study, I knew that I was living in a brighter day. Because I didn't have an exact moment that marked that realization, I told God in prayer one day that I knew Jesus was his son and that he died on the cross to pay the penalty for my sins and that I wanted to be in relationship with him and keep growing into the person he wanted me to be.

I used the language given to me in the Bible study to tell God what I already believed.

That's what "confessing our faith" means. Telling God we recognize our need for Jesus in our lives. It's a prayer of surrender that places us in a permanent relationship with Jesus, here on earth now and eternally in heaven. We begin a faith journey with a new destination, and Jesus lights our path all the way home.

Once we begin this faith journey, we experience many memorable, illuminating moments. My friend Robyn Randall describes one of hers that came through her first pregnancy test. She writes,

When I thought I might be pregnant with our first child, I knew I felt different. I wasn't at the point of nausea or bouts of crying for no reason. To this day, I can't explain what motivated me to take a test. I just felt different. And so I did, and I waited . . . and waited . . . and waited. And in just two minutes, my life changed forever.

I was going to be a mom.

We were going to be parents.

Two minutes before, it was just me. Two minutes later, I knew there was an existence, a human growing inside of me. While no physical developments changed in those two minutes, my mind was convinced that I was pregnant because the test said there was a baby in me. My doctor confirmed it.

I couldn't see him.

I couldn't feel him.

I couldn't talk to him.

Yet I believed that I was pregnant. I took their word for it. I accepted it by faith. And suddenly I had this window of understanding into my acceptance of God. The writer of the book of Hebrews said, "[Faith] is the evidence of things we cannot yet see" (Hebrews 11:1 NLT).

Even when we can't see or feel Jesus, faith gives us the assurance he is there because we know conception has occurred. And faith begins to light our way home—in the dark.

We have that assurance every time we experience longings. The longing for understanding. Love. Joy. Peace. Hope. Light. I'm now convinced that God has a purpose for those longings. He could wipe them out of our lives once and for all, but when we continue to experience them, we continue to turn back to Jesus, who understands. He is love and joy and peace. He gives us hope; he is the light of the world (John 8:12); he will light our path (Ps. 119:105); and he is making his light shine in our hearts (2 Cor. 4:6). He lights our way home to a place where we will live with him forever.

Faith of a Child

When our children were young, I prayed that we would be able to love our children as Jesus loves us, and that by letting his love shine through us, they would be drawn to him. I prayed that we might light their way home to Jesus by being vulnerable and real and showing our need for and dependence upon him. That's the ultimate and greatest purpose of our family. Lynn and I want to point them to something beyond ourselves.

Surely we hope they will always turn to us and each other for love and fun and loyalty and motivation to grow. But that is not an end in itself. Our purpose is not to pose for a "Happy Family Portrait" to hang above the mantel for all to admire. It is to be a family of faith, to point each other—and others—to Jesus. To find the way home and then be the lights that illuminate that pathway for others.

We've heard the familiar saying that "God has no grandchildren." The message is that faith comes to each generation by each person's personal choices. Though we can't control those holy moments of choice, we do influence what our children learn about faith, which starts at home.

According to researcher George Barna (in his online report from November 17, 2003), whose company tracks

---

Family is …
Where God teaches you about his love.

---

religious behavior nationally, a person's moral foundations are in place by age nine. This underscores the importance of families, not churches, taking the lead in the spiritual development of children. In families where children became mature Christians, evidence showed that churches partnered with parents, encouraging and equipping them to develop their children spiritually. The families provided a faith-based context for security, belonging, spiritual and moral education, and accountability.

Moms make a difference in this process. At MOPS International, we hear many stories about mothers who come to know Jesus at MOPS, and their whole family follows. One mom wrote that she grew up in a family that didn't go to church. She started attending MOPS as the mother of a three- and a six-year-old. In the midst of hearing talks about nutrition, financial planning, and parenting, she learned about the source of hope for a mom. "I came to the Lord because of the joy and strength I saw in the lives of my MOPS friends. . . .

My daughter also accepted Jesus; then my son; and eventually my husband."

One mother of adult children wrote about her regret that she didn't do a better job teaching her children about God and faith when they were preschoolers. "Faith in God doesn't just happen, no matter how many Sundays you spend in Sunday school. You have to talk about God and bring him into every aspect of your lives."

One thing I'm learning in this season of life with adult children: we all have regrets about the way we parented yesterday or last week or five years ago, but hear me on this—it is never . . . *never* . . . NEVER too late to make a difference in the life of your child, no matter the age.

A child's hunger for God: A child's ability to grasp spiritual concepts changes significantly as he or she grows up. During the preschool years, children view God much as they do Santa Claus: unreal and magical. They cannot yet comprehend the meaning of death and resurrection, because for them, death is pretend and temporary. They play dead in their games. Then they get up and go on to another game.

They eagerly devour Bible stories. Children ages two to five have simple, trusting faith, and truth is anything we tell them. They don't reason, but they can begin to appreciate the idea of trusting God's promises by experiencing the reality they know: night follows day and spring follows winter, just as God promises.

As children reach age five or six, they can experience tremendous spiritual growth. They begin to think more conceptually and move away from the fantasy concept of God. They understand more about faith and grace and that God doesn't always answer our prayers exactly as we ask. This is the time many children ask Jesus into their lives. A fifth grader at our church gave her testimony, which profoundly describes that decision in her life.

For a long time, I thought I was born a Christian because my parents were Christians. Then I learned that I had to ask Jesus into my heart myself. That didn't sound too hard. So one night before bed, when I was six years old, I asked Jesus into my heart.

Both my parents were with me, and we prayed together, and then I went to sleep. When I woke up, I didn't feel any different, and I didn't notice that anything in my life changed.

It wasn't until this year that I began to realize I could pray and talk to Jesus all by myself, every morning and all during the day. I could pray for thirty seconds or five minutes, anytime, anywhere. That's when I began to understand the meaning of a personal relationship with the Lord.

A child's experience of God's presence: During the preschool years, we try to highlight the reality of Jesus in the everyday moments of our lives. Some moms describe the ways they do this:

- "Whenever we're outside, we notice how incredibly wonderful God made the world. We lie on the grass and spot a perfect little ladybug. We watch the waves or hike in the mountains or look at the stars."

- "We pray to Jesus every night with our two-and-a-half-year-old. Not only for our family. For all the animals in the world, ice cream, VeggieTales (especially Larryboy), his favorite stuffed animals, blueberries. I think he uses it as a stalling technique so he doesn't have to go to bed right away, but what a great technique!"

- "I try to show my children the love of Jesus by taking time for what's important to them and meeting them where they are, as he did with the people he met."

- "Each morning as we drive my husband to work (we're a one-car family), we drive over Hallelujah Hill. At that point we know it's time to pray for our day. We pray conversationally for people and circumstances that need God's touch; we praise God for all he's given us. It's neat to hear our children pray and trust God completely."

- "I pray with my four- and two-year-olds all day long. When we hear a siren, we pray for whoever is in trouble. We pray for patience when Mommy's having a bad day. My two-year-old was sitting on the potty, and I heard her ask Jesus to help her 'get the potty out.'"

- "We praise God often, thanking him for our fun, our blessings, and one another. What matters most to me and our family is preparing each other to live in his family forever."

These are moms who are lighting the way home for their children.

Faith of a Family

What matters most in expressing faith as a family? I asked our three adult children this question, and these are their answers.

Sunday matters: Each day of the week has its own personality. Monday is get-up-and-go day. Friday is fun day. Saturday is sleep-late day. Sunday . . . well, Sunday was different in our family. "It was the only day we all got up and went to the same place for the same reason," one of our daughters said. At church we became part of a larger family of people who worshipped and praised God and prayed together. "But you didn't just take us to Sunday school. You also taught Sunday school, which helped us know that we were part of something that mattered." Another stated that "what we did on Sunday made the rest of the week better."

Being real matters: Our kids did not want to be part of a "perfect-looking Christian family wearing fake smiles and living in la-la land." No problem. We were far from perfect, and if Lynn or I ever thought we were even close to "having it all together," our children quickly pulled us back to reality. Part of God's miraculous plan of matching parents and children includes this fact that children keep us—and our faith—real.

Our children weren't interested in a faith that was about a bunch of rigid rules and "doing" all the right things. They were drawn to a faith that was about relationships. "Rules without relationship turn me away from faith, and I didn't want to see God as a fear factor," one said. This is crucial, because faith and religion can be confusing to a child. Another said, "We knew we could have faith and still have fun." Faith wasn't about control. "We had the freedom to develop our own faith. We had opportunities to go to youth group and camp, but you didn't force us into those activities."

Prayer matters: Here's a confession. We didn't have regular family devotions, but our children remember many spontaneous holy moments, talking about God and to God in everyday places. Our kids remember saying grace, "but we also prayed together at other times, like whenever a child had a problem or when we felt afraid." Lindsay remembers praying on a ski slope when she was about eight years old. She and I had taken a wrong turn and ended up on a black diamond (expert) slope instead of a green triangle (easiest) slope. I can still remember the panic we felt as we realized there was no way out except straight down. We turned our "yikes attack" into a prayer, and soon two ski patrolmen appeared and guided us down the mountain.

Our children also knew their parents prayed regularly for them. When they were young, I fell into the daily habit of praying for them as Jesus prayed for his disciples (John 17:6–26). I still pray this way today, and I call it my "five-finger prayer," because I hold up one finger for each person in the family, including my niece who sometimes lived with us in the summers when our kids were growing up. I now add their spouses and children to their finger. In my own paraphrase, I pray that

> They will be protected—both physically and spiritually. Physically in their safety as they go from place to place. Spiritually so that God's truth protects them from anything that is not from him, such as discouragement or fear or lack of confidence.
>
> They will seek his will and make choices according to his will, and that those choices will grow them into the people he's created them to be, in his image.
>
> They will have a godly person to walk alongside them and support them when they grow weary and point them back to Jesus if they get off track.

Freedom to be matters: This is my own addition to our kids' list about the expression of faith in a family. Our children don't naturally inherit our faith. They have to own it for themselves, and one of the dangers of growing up in a Christian home is that we may not give them the opportunity to do this. We have the right instincts. Their faith choices matter so much to us that we end up controlling the way they express their faith without realizing how this can stunt their growth.

While we may require our children to attend church with us and build a foundation of faith early in their lives, by the time they reach their teenage years, that foundation is set, and making too many requirements at that stage can become a control factor that shuts down the growth of their faith. I have a friend whose sixteen-year-old son is attending a different church at the moment, and some of this mom's Christian friends think that's terrible. Researcher George Barna tells us, in his November 17, 2003, online report, that the biggest number of people drop out of church between the ages of eighteen and twenty-four. Is this partly because we don't allow them to ask honest questions, explore their questions, and own their own faith?

Two of our three children attended Christian colleges and said that many kids in the freshman class fled from their faith because it was the first time in their lives they experienced any freedom to consider what their faith meant to them. Up until that time, their faith had been a response to requirements. My friend whose son is attending a differ-

---

Family means . . .

You are part of something bigger than you.

---

ent church says that "it makes me a little sad that we can't worship all together, but it makes me more joyful that he is following God of his own volition and choosing to go to a church where the worship style suits his expression of worshipping God (rather than just choosing not to go to church)."

What about the kids who seem to drop out in this season and leave their faith behind them? What does God do with them? He assures us that he keeps calling them back, like the shepherd who leaves the flock to pursue the one lost lamb. I know many Christian parents who pray with the hope that the love of Jesus poured into their children's hearts is still there and will eventually light their way home.

Faith Shines Like a Star

The reality of faith brightens and deepens the expression of each of the other five-star qualities we've already discussed. Consider how our relationship with Jesus and the hope we have in him shines through each one of the qualities:

Love: Faith deepens our understanding of love and helps us love the unlovely—in ourselves and in others—because he first loved us.

Fun: Faith gives us joy in experiencing his original intent to celebrate all that is good and praising him for all the good he gives us.

Loyalty: Faith helps us understand our free will. We get to choose God and then choose forgiveness and then choose commitment in our relationships.

Growth: Faith puts a desire in our hearts to grow closer to God's image and grow his character in us. He loves us where we are but loves us too much to leave us where we are. His character includes love, joy, peace, patience, kindness, goodness, gentleness, faithfulness, and self-control.

Faith: Faith gives us the perspective to embrace and enjoy all that life brings. Faith gives deeper meaning to all our circumstances. Faith lights our way home and becomes a light for others to find that way home.

As we experience and express these qualities in our families, we naturally reflect these qualities to others. Have you ever wondered what others see?

What do your neighbors know about your family? What about us tells others who we are? Our cars? Our bumper stickers? Our relationships? I was walking our dog through our neighborhood on garbage day recently, and it struck me that as neighbors, our garbage might reveal the most we know about each other. Those bins reveal what we read, what we buy, what we eat and drink, to name just a few characteristics. But don't we hope our neighbors know more about who we are and what matters most to us?

Mother Teresa said, "We will never know how much good just a simple smile can do. We tell people how kind, forgiving and understanding God is—are we the living proof? Can they really see the kindness, this forgiveness, this understanding, alive in us?"

I'd like our family to be known in our neighborhood like my friend Beth's family is known in hers. Her son was a stu-

---

"The only thing that counts is faith expressing itself through love."
~ Galatians 5:6

---

dent at Columbine on the day that etched that high school into our minds forever. The day when thirteen people were killed by two students who went on a horrifying shooting rampage through the school. Her son Andrew and some other students escaped to a small room where they scrunched down on the floor, hiding for hours, while the school's alarm system blared, the sprinkling systems went off, and the place was in utter chaos. Andrew and his fellow students didn't know if the killers would burst into their room at any moment.

I was in a meeting with Beth when she heard the news. She rushed to the place where they were evacuating the students rescued from the school. She waited in agony for hours until the last bus pulled into that parking lot. Was Andrew on that bus? Her heart pounded loudly . . . until she saw him.

Families reeled from the shock and pain that day. That night Beth's family gathered in their home, watching television, praying for the other families, and thanking God for each other. There was a knock on the door. Another Columbine father and son stood there, looking bewildered.

"We saw your porch light on, and we just needed to talk." Beth and her husband invited them in and spent the next hour trying to help this father and son make sense out of a senseless situation.

This father and son knew Beth's family, and like moths to the light, they came to their front door. They hoped this family could show them the way through a dark place. They knew this family had faith.

Oh, that our families can offer such a light. That we might be beacons of light for each other—and others in our larger world. Not because we have all the answers, but because we know the one who does. And that in knowing him, we might shine like stars in the universe and light the way home.

Wonderings

1. How do you identify with Robyn Randall's comparison of accepting her pregnancy test results to accepting God . . . both by faith? (See page 177.)
2. What are some of the longings in your heart today? Where do you turn to satisfy those longings?
3. Our hope is to grow a family that "shines like a star in the universe." What does this mean to you? What do you think your family reflects to others? In what

ways are you becoming a family that "lights the way home"?

4. Use this space to write a prayer for your family. A Mother's Prayer:

_____

_____

_____

_____

_____

Resources

Reading to our children is a family activity that builds relationships. Here's a list of books that help the whole family understand some messages of faith.

The Legend of the Easter Egg by Lori Walburg, Zonderkidz.

The Legend of the Candy Cane by Lori Walburg, Zonderkidz. (Both have great gospel presentations.)

You Are Special by Max Lucado, Crossway Books.

Just the Way I Am by Max Lucado, Crossway Books.

It's Not Funny, I've Lost My Money by Melody Carlson, Crossway Books. (This tells the parable of the lost coin.)

Love Your Neighbor by Melody Carlson, Broadman and Holman. (A kid learns to love his neighbor, Matt. 22:39.)

Does God Know How to Tie Shoes? by Nancy White Carlstrom, Eerdmans.

The Legend of the Three Trees, from the screenplay by George Taweel and Rob Loos, based on the traditional folk tale, Tommy Nelson.

A Child's First Book of Prayers by Lois Rock and Alison Jay, Augsburg Books. (This is great to read at mealtime; it has prayers for all kinds of things and situations and great illustrations.)

Read with Me Bible, Zonderkidz. (This has great illustrations.)

Little Jesus, Little Me. (This is a MOPS book, great for infants to two-year-olds.)

9

Full-Circle Families

The Sunday afternoon seemed like the perfect ending to a near-perfect family weekend. Of course I had no idea that I would relive each moment of this day, searching for any clues that might have forecasted what was about to happen.

We'd gathered with two of our three children, their spouses, and our granddaughter to enjoy the first few days of summer in Steamboat Springs, high in the Colorado mountains. Early that morning, our son, Derek, had run a half-marathon, and now we were celebrating, sitting in a circle around a table on the patio at a streamside restaurant.

We passed ten-month-old Gabriella around the circle, delighting in this first child of a new generation in our family. She especially loved Lynn, her Opa ("grandpa" in Dutch). Sitting on his lap, she opened her arms wide and clapped her hands in sheer joy. When the food came, Lynn said a quick, open-eyed prayer (his way of saying grace at a restaurant), thanking God for the food, the blessing of being together, and for Gabriella (who was already learning to listen for her name in a prayer).

For me, sitting across the table, this seemed a holy moment. From the time our children were Gabi's age, I hoped we would enjoy being together as adults like this, not out of obligation, but out of desire. I hoped they would grow up to marry people exactly as each had, and that we'd be blessed with grandchildren like Gabi, who cared about hearing her name said in a prayer.

Yes, this seemed a holy moment, because if I've learned anything in all these years of parenting, I've learned there are no guarantees. We pour our best (and sometimes our not-so-best) into the lives of our children; we try to pass on what we know to be true about faith and hope ... but we don't control the results.

I tried to do the mom part. Bedtime prayers at tuck-in time. Playing kids' praise songs really loud as I drove them places in the car. And I had what they considered an annoying habit of writing Bible verses on sticky notes and placing them on the refrigerator door or their pillows or the mirrors in their bathroom.

When do you know whether anything on those sticky notes stuck? When does the invisible become visible?

I do know that as I sat there streamside on that beautiful June afternoon, I felt an overwhelming wave of gratitude for our family.

The next morning, we all jumped out of bed early to get back down the mountain to our jobs. Kendall and David left at 6 a.m. The rest of us piled into our car a couple of hours later, and we stopped for gas before starting our trek back to Boulder. Lynn had just finished pumping gas when he looked a bit bewildered.

"I have a terrible headache," he said.

He stumbled trying to get back in the car, and I knew in an instant this was not a normal headache. We quickly found our way to the local emergency room, where we soon learned that Lynn's headache was caused by a life-threatening bleed in his brain. His brain was swelling quickly, and he needed surgery immediately in order to survive. The ER doctor made arrangements to fly him back to the hospital in Boulder where a brain surgeon would be waiting.

They told me I could fly with Lynn if I promised not to become a patient also. They then advised Derek and his wife, Alexandra, to tell Lynn anything they needed him to know, even though he was losing consciousness. Their message was clear. They were not sure he would make it through the flight.

There was a moment when I didn't think he had. I sat in the front of that small plane, practically knee-to-knee with the pilot. The engine was so loud, there was no expectation of conversation. I kept turning around to check on Lynn, who was strapped to a gurney with a paramedic on each side. They kept checking various monitors and adjusting tubes. I could see only one monitor, and as the plane flew over the jagged mountain peaks, the line on its screen zigzagged . . . and then went flat. The paramedics wouldn't look at me. It wasn't until we landed that they gave me a thumbs-up. Lynn had survived the flight.

He was wheeled into brain surgery immediately, and when the doctor finally emerged six hours later, he reported that Lynn was in critical condition with extensive brain damage. I reeled at what the doctor's words might mean.

Two days later, Lynn was rushed back into emergency surgery because his brain started swelling again. The doctor then put him in a drug-induced coma on life support in intensive care. Would he survive? If he did, how much of Lynn would return, due to his brain injury? The doctors seemed reluctant to give us hope.

A week later, the doctor finally began to bring Lynn out of the coma, and he was responsive to us but had absolutely no feeling or movement on his whole left side. Derek and Alex brought Gabriella to the hospital and held her up outside his window where she began to clap for her Opa. We told Lynn that he had to learn to clap again, just like Gabi. Over the next several days, he worked so hard to move his little finger and finally his hand—until he could clap, just like Gabi.

Slowly Lynn became more and more responsive. He was moved to a rehab center where he learned to walk again, and a few weeks later, he came home, where he continued to make a miraculous recovery. He is now back at work at his law firm and doing most normal things, but our family will never be the same.

Those days of waiting when Lynn was in the coma seemed so endless. I was grateful that our children all gathered at our house, because I felt afraid. And the most amazing thing started happening . . . sticky notes with Bible verses—in their handwriting—began to appear on the refrigerator door. And on my mirror. As they drove me back and forth to the hospital, they played praise music in the car. Really loud! And before I fell in bed at night, they prayed with me, when I couldn't pray by myself. From the reservoir of their own faith, they poured hope and love back into me during those long days of waiting and wondering.

We looked death right in the face, and God answered our prayer. Yet he didn't say, "Lynn won't die." He simply said, "Not yet." As we savor life in the "not yet," Lynn and I are greatly comforted by the gift of a glimpse of what will live beyond us. The invisible became visible by the faith our children showed during this crisis and the way they passed hope back to us in the midst of our fears. They became like shining stars offering light in a scary, dark place.

This full-circle story will become part of our family history.

Full Circles

A family comes full circle when the things that matter most are received, passed on, and passed back or beyond—by the next generation. Not out of guilt or obligation. Out of their own personal desire and ownership. Something shows that they get it (whatever "it" is) and it lives inside their own hearts. It becomes part of who they are, and by their choices or words or actions, they make the invisible visible.

It might be turning birthdays into big-deal ways to honor people; making biscuit gravy the way Grandma used to because that matters to Grandma, who can't make it anymore; forgiving a brother or cousin or parent, not because the person earns or deserves it, but because that's the way God treats us; reading the Bible in bed at night, even when the tuck-in parent isn't home; or putting sticky notes with Bible verses on the refrigerator door.

It means experiencing the five-star qualities of love, fun, loyalty, growth, and faith—and expressing those qualities in visible ways.

One of my favorite full-circle stories about love is described in the popular children's book *Love You Forever* by Robert Munsch. It's the story of a mother's love for her child and the way that love is passed down through generations. It begins with the mom rocking her baby to sleep singing this simple, sweet lullaby.

I'll love you forever,
I'll like you for always,
As long as I'm living
my baby you'll be.

She faithfully sings the song throughout her child's life, from toddler to rebellious adolescent to grown young man. Her words seem invisibly poured into him in all these different seasons. Finally she grows too old and sick to sing it, and she calls her son, who comes and rocks her and sings the song back to her. And then returns home to sing the lullaby to his newborn little girl.

The invisible becomes visible in a full-circle love story.

With full circles, we get a bigger-picture view of the ongoing-ness of the family. We see the generations overlapping and the importance of passing on what matters most.

Full-circle moments don't happen quickly in a family. They simmer invisibly over ho-hum mornings around the kitchen counter, afternoons seat belted into the car, and before-bed conversations at the end of a day. Then, Wow! You suddenly catch a glimpse of one. The invisible becomes visible—and you ponder the memory in your heart.

Remembering and Reminding

Moms play a special role in this ongoing process. Though I'm not much into gender stereotypes, I know that God gives mothers hearts for pondering, which equip us for our part in these full circles. We become Remember-ers and Reminders. We see a powerful example in the description of Mary's heart. When Jesus was born in that stable in Bethlehem, so much happened so quickly . . . angels and shepherds coming and going, and everyone telling Mary everything they'd heard about her baby. In the midst of it all, we learn that "Mary kept all these things and pondered them in her heart" (Luke 2:19 KJV). She gathered all the words and memories and held them safely in her heart. She pondered them as she sought to be the best mom she could be. She remembered them; they reminded her who Jesus was. She held on to those memories as the invisible became visible.

Moms seem wired to be Remember-ers. We feel and remember emotions more than most males. It's been said that men never remember marital spats and women never forget them. I can give an "amen" to that. I can look at a picture taken on a family vacation ten years ago and remember that Lynn and I weren't getting along at that moment because we were both worried the vacation was costing us too much money. He has no such memory of those feelings and doesn't like that I do.

All this remembering is intended for good, in God's purposes. As moms, we can be Remember-ers and Reminders for our families. From their infancy, we begin to catch glimpses of who our children are, especially their unique strengths. We gather these memories and store them in our hearts so we can be Reminders.

I particularly remember a phone call from Derek years ago when he needed some reminders. He had graduated from college and was living alone and looking for a job in social work far away from home. Nothing was working out, and he was discouraged. "I'm starting to wonder if I'm going in the wrong direction," he said.

As we talked, I remembered some of the ponderings in my heart. I saw a six-year-old boy tenderly helping his barefoot little sister across a prickly meadow. A ten-year-old passing the soccer ball off to a teammate in a tournament. A sixteen-year-old persevering through a frustrating basketball season. And a college student choosing best friends who wanted to be in a Bible study together. I saw a sensitive, determined boy growing into a compassionate and faithful young man. Out of these ponderings, I could remind him of the qualities God had planted in his soul, which have been growing since he was a child. I could remind him that God promises to complete the good work he starts in each of us. I could help keep this full circle growing.

I knew a mom who was a hospice patient in the last stages of pancreatic cancer and was determined to pass her

---

Family is . . .
A soft place to land.

---

ponderings on to each of her five sons in the form of blessings before she died. They were all in their twenties; only one was married. She wanted to leave each of them with a reminder of what she had seen in them. So she spent time alone with each son, telling them what characteristics she had seen in them, reminding them of the kind of husband or daddy she knew they would become one day. The day after she passed her blessing on to her fifth son, she died.

Ingrid Trobisch is a mother, grandmother, former missionary, and author of several books, including *Keeper of the Springs*, which is the title she claims for herself. A "Keeper of the Springs" is someone who keeps the springs clean and sees that others get enough fresh, life-giving water. She sees herself as a "keeper" for her children and grandchildren. She keeps memories, treasures, history, beauty, both tangibles and intangibles. She stores them in her heart and in her childhood homestead where she lives.

God asks us to be Remember-ers and Reminders, Keepers of the Springs for the next generation. As the psalmist writes,

We will tell the next generation
the praiseworthy deeds of the LORD,
his power, and the wonders he has done. . . .

So the next generation would know them,
even the children yet to be born,
and they in turn would tell their children.

Then they would put their trust in God
and would not forget his deeds
but would keep his commands.

Psalm 78:4, 6–7

When we are Remember-ers and Reminders, we keep the full circle going.

A Party to Remember

I hosted a Remembering Party not long ago. Actually, my daughter-in-law, Alexandra, hosted it for me. She and I have the same birthday, which I think is a God-given gift of coincidence. This year, our birthdays fell on a Sunday; it was her thirtieth, and she celebrated by competing in a minitriathlon. (I toyed with the idea of joining her in that physical challenge but toyed and tarried until registration was closed. What a shame!) Derek planned a party to honor his wife's feat, which I thought was a great idea (and I had great fun at her party!). Alex decided I still needed my own party, so for my birthday gift, she gave me an I.O.U. for a party. "You pick the theme, guest list, and place—and I'll take care of the rest." What a deal!

I loved considering all the possibilities. A small, cozy dinner party? A Sunday brunch? Since I was immersed in the topic of five-star families for this book, I finally decided to invite three generations—moms, daughters, and grand-children—for a late summer afternoon gathering on our patio to talk about families.

The party invitation, sprinkled with whimsical stars, read

Please join us for a
Mother-Daughter FAC
(Friends and Conversation)
Topic: What Matters Most in Your Family?

Alex prepared fabulous food from Spain, in honor of her father, who lives there. Spanish tortillas. Meatballs. White-bean salad. Asparagus with prosciutto. Roasted, salted almonds. The table was decorated with flowers, stars, and candles. She got a babysitter to help with the little ones, and we gathered on our patio, three generations of women, ranging in age from sixty down to about six months. We expected to have fun and good conversation. We got so much more! As we talked about love and loyalty, fun, faith, and the freedom to grow, mothers and daughters mined rich memories out of each other.

"I'm glad you allowed us to be different, Mom."

"We celebrated Christmas well . . . family caroling party and the way you chose a unique wrapping paper for each of us and wrapped all our presents in it."

"You respected our choices."

"We went on those great car trips where we were all together but away from home."

"Dad made up stories about Peter and Jimmy Rabbit and their mother, Welsh Rabbit."

"Peach Chair Time . . ." and the conversation stopped, because no one knew what this young mom meant . . . except her other sister and her mother.

"Whenever one of us felt a little sad," she continued, "we got some snuggle time with Mom on the peach-colored chair in her bedroom."

"I haven't thought of 'Peach Chair Time' forever," her mother responded. "I got that chair right after my brother died of cancer in his early twenties, and I needed a comforting place to go when I felt sad. Then when I became a mom, I took my girls to that chair and rocked them when they felt sad."

"You know what?" her daughter added. "We now have a big, brown, comfy chair at home, and when my little one feels sad, we sit together there and have some Big Brown Chair Time."

A full-circle story of something given, received, and passed on, from one generation to another and another, so the circle continues.

"We have a 'hugs and kisses' tradition," another mother added. "When a family member is leaving for a time, they find that chocolate candy in their shoes or suitcase or whatever. When our daughter got married recently, she and her new husband stopped by our house to pick up their luggage while we were still at the reception. When we arrived home, we opened our front door, and there were candy kisses all over the stairway. I cried because the message was: they're on their own but still part of the family."

A full-circle story of a tradition passed on and passed back.

The afternoon of remembering went on, with descriptions of how faith helped a mom through the pain of facing some difficult childhood memories; how families learned love and loyalty through divorce, and health crises and problems with children, and the humor and fun that holds us all together. As the sun started to set and the kids got tired, we wrapped up our conversation. What surprised me was the outpouring of gratitude from our guests for the opportunity to simply remember what's stored in their hearts and think about the ways they've tried to express the qualities of love, fun, loyalty, growth, and faith in their families. To recall their own full-circle stories.

"We have all these memories hidden deep in our souls, waiting to be remembered," one mom commented, "but we so rarely take the time to access them."

Later that night, Lynn and I sat out on that same patio, sharing some leftovers from the party as I told him about the many conversations. Of course, we talked about our own family. How appropriate that we could see the first evening

---

Family is . . .
Something you take with you, wherever you go.

---

star just beginning to twinkle in the summer-evening sky. Like the invisible North Star becoming visible.

We're living in the season that we always aimed for. We've grown our children into adults, which is the goal of every family. But it's about so much more than that. We poured ourselves into their lives as best as we knew how. But it's about more than that. Way back so many years ago, as we stood at the beginning of this family journey, we thought about the qualities that we wanted our family to experience and express.

I remember what we wanted:

Love: To be a family that loved each other with sensitivity and awareness.

Fun: To have fun—so our children wanted to spend time together.

Loyalty: To choose to be loyal and committed to each other. Connected . . . for always.

Growth: To encourage the freedom to keep growing and changing.

Faith: To reflect the hope we have in God—and shine like a bright star in the nighttime sky, so that others might see that hope.

These were the five-star qualities that gave us something to aim toward. Qualities always before us and beckoning us to reach beyond ourselves for goals not yet reached.

"We didn't do it all right," I said to Lynn as I scraped the last bit of the Spanish tortillas off the plate.

"But we've got lots to be thankful for," he added.

From the patio where we sat, I could see through to the kitchen, where the sticky notes with Scriptures were still on the refrigerator door.

Like the fact that those sticky notes stuck.

Legacies left that will shine into the next generation.

Wonderings

1. Can you describe a full-circle moment in your family —when the invisible became visible?
2. In what ways are you a Reminder for your children? How do you remind them of who you know them to be?
3. The psalmist tells us to tell the next generation of the wonders God has done, so that they will believe. And their children will believe. What wonders has God done in your life? Have you passed this story on? Why or why not?
4. How about hosting your own FAC (Friends and Conversation) party? Here are some questions to bounce around a circle of friends or answer for yourself.

Love: meets our greatest needs.

Question: How did you know you were loved, growing up? What's your favorite way to communicate love to your children?

Fun: makes us want to be together.

Question: What did your family do for fun? Any unique traditions from your original family that you are still carrying on today?

Loyalty: connects us . . . for always.

Question: What does loyalty mean to you, and how do you promote loyalty?

Growth: keeps us healthy.

Question: How do you make room for change and growth in your family?

Faith: lights our way home.

Question: Why does faith matter in your family, and how are you passing it on?

Epilogue

My daughter Lindsay just had her baby.

Karis, they named her. It's the Greek word for "grace."

She and Jeff chose that name many months ago, shortly after the doctor studied their ultrasound and pronounced her a girl. From that moment, they began talking to her and caressing her from the outside in.

They decorated the nursery in pastels and filled the drawers with little-girl clothes.

And now Karis is here, all seven-and-one-half pounds of her.

I know every detail of her birth because I videotaped it. (And I did a good job!) Because I watched her take her first breath, I feel a special bond to her.

It's the middle of the night now, and I'm rocking her, so that her mommy and daddy can get some sleep. She's only five days old and hasn't quite figured out the difference between day and night.

As I fold her tiny fingers over mine, I gaze into her deep blue eyes. I feel like I've known her for a long time. Yet I also yearn to know her. Who she is . . . who she'll become. She blinks, as if searching for something familiar. Something secure in this new world.

She starts getting fussy, so I walk her around the darkened house, pausing at a window where I hold her up to the night sky.

"Can you see the twinkling stars in the darkness, Baby?"

I snuggle her close, sing a lullaby ... and then say a prayer.

> Twinkle, twinkle, little star,
> How I wonder what you are.
> Up above the world so high,
> Like a diamond in the sky.
> Twinkle, twinkle, little star,
> How I wonder what you are.

Dear Jesus,

Hold this precious baby close to your heart. Cherish and protect her and grow her strong in this family you've chosen for her. Bless her parents with your wisdom and tenderness. May they give her both a safe and a stretching place from which to grow and wonder—and discover what matters most in her life.

May she grow to know you, Jesus.

Amen.

Acknowledgments

The words on all the preceding pages come from the influence, wisdom, and encouragement of many people. I want to thank some of them on this page.

First my own growing family—my husband, Lynn, our children and their spouses, Derek and Alexandra, Lindsay and Jeff, and Kendall and David, and their children. All Five-Star in my book!

My siblings and their families: Joan, Dexter, and Mark. And my parents. For many good memories and great loyalty.

My friends and co-workers at MOPS International, especially Elisa Morgan, Beth Lagerborg, and Carla Foote who read and re-read endlessly. Also Brenda Quinn and Stacie Maslyn.

My many friends and MOPS moms who shared their family stories and memories.

My prayer partners who talked to God faithfully on my behalf.

Rick Christian and Lee Hough at Alive Communications for perseverance and advocacy.

Jennifer Leep, Twila Bennett, Stephanie Vink, and many others on the team at Revell for the pursuit of excellence.

And many, many others whom I will continue to remember and be grateful for as I think about what matters most . . . and how a family grows from good to great!

Carol Kuykendall has served as director of strategic projects of MOPS International (Mothers of Preschoolers), an outreach ministry with thirty-five hundred groups reaching more than one hundred thousand women worldwide. Carol has authored or coauthored nine books on family and women's issues. She also writes for *Guideposts* and *Daily Guideposts*, and her articles have appeared in *Reader's Digest* and *Parents* magazines. She is a popular seminar and retreat speaker and has been a guest on the *Today Show* and the *Focus on the Family* and *Family Life Today* radio broadcasts.

Carol and her husband, Lynn, recently celebrated their thirty-seventh wedding anniversary and are living in the "grandfamily" season of life with their three grown children and their spouses and children. Becoming Oma and Opa ("grandmother and grandfather" in Dutch) is one of God's great blessings and gives them yet another opportunity to celebrate the wonders of childhood.

Carol graduated from the University of Colorado with a bachelor's degree in journalism. She and Lynn live in Boulder, Colorado.

About MOPS

You take care of your children, Mom. Who takes care of you? MOPS International (Mothers of Preschoolers) encourages, equips, and develops every mother of a preschooler to be the best mom she can be.

MOPS International is dedicated to the message that "mothering matters" and understands that moms of young children (ages infancy to kindergarten) need encouragement during these critical and formative years. Chartered MOPS groups meet in approximately four thousand churches and Christian ministries throughout the United States and twenty-four other countries. Each MOPS group program helps mothers find friendship and acceptance, provides opportunities for women to develop and practice leadership skills in a group, and promotes spiritual growth. There are various types of MOPS groups to meet every mother of a preschooler right where she is in life. These groups meet during the daytime, in the evenings, and on weekends; in churches, in homes, and in workplaces.

The MOPPETS program offers a loving, learning experience for children while their moms attend MOPS. Other quality MOPS resources include *MOMSense* magazine, books for moms (available at www.MOPShop.org), website forums, and events.

With 14.3 million mothers of preschoolers in the United States alone, many moms can't attend a MOPS group.

However, these moms still need the mothering support that MOPS International can offer! For a small registration fee, any mother of a preschooler can join the MOPS International Membership and receive *MOMSense* magazine six times a year, a weekly MOM-E-Mail of encouragement, and other valuable benefits.

Get Connected!
www.MOPS.org